BAKING
WITH
WHOLE GRAINS

BAKING WITH
WHOLE GRAINS

Cookies, Cakes, Scones, Pies, Pizza, Breads, and More!

Valerie Baer

Good Books

New York, New York

Contents

Introduction

When I was growing up, my family always had a garden. We tried to eat healthy—we took that for granted, although we weren't experts on nutrition. We just ate whatever was in season in the garden, and we ate what we preserved from our garden the rest of the year. It was delicious, and we loved the food, but I must say, it all seemed very ordinary.

My dad was a reader, and I remember that he became very sensitive to the fact that our daily choices now will affect many people besides ourselves, including our children and grandchildren. He and my mom instilled in all of us that people and our environment are damaged if we aren't careful.

We weren't saints. But we were taught to live responsibly when we were little. My dad continued to influence me, even after I was grown up. I can bring back a moment about thirty years ago after I had my first child. We were sitting together and talking, and he noticed a plastic milk jug that was sitting nearby. "You know," he said, "that will still be around 500 years from now." It was a light bulb moment for me. Even now I make our own pancake syrup because store-bought syrup comes in plastic bottles.

Even though a garden was always part of my life, I didn't love gardening! But as our children grew older and I had more time, I began to discover the fun (and frustration) of raising our own food. For the most part, I enjoy growing and preserving a good portion of the food that we eat now. My mom still gardens at age eighty. She recently told me, "I sit down to a meal and I

think, I grew most of this myself!"

Occasionally we have our neighboring farmer plant soft grain wheat on a parcel of our land. In exchange, we get to dip a few years' supply of grain from the harvesters' storage bin. The wheat needs to be washed, dried, and frozen for a week or two in order to store it long-term. I love grinding it as I need it for baking.

I was twelve or thirteen when our aunt introduced us to baking our own whole grain bread. Suddenly it was clear that white flour has the best parts taken out of it. I helped make our family's bread—and I became really interested in using the whole of everything whenever I could. Baking yeast breads went well for me, but I didn't do so well at working whole grains into pancakes and waffles and other non-yeast baked things.

Then one day, my sister Carmen started grinding her own soft wheat. And when she used it in her baked goods, the results were wonderful! She helped me begin to crack open some of the mysteries about which flours to use for which kinds of baked goods. Suddenly everything we baked with the soft grain was lighter than what we had made before. And I wasn't getting gripes about my baked things being too heavy.

Now on Sunday evenings, when our kids all come home, what do they want me to make? Whole wheat waffles, topped with homemade yogurt or fruit, fresh or frozen, depending on the time of year. Sometimes we add canned fruit, applesauce, or nuts.

My little granddaughter, who eats mostly whole grain foods, stayed overnight at a friend's house. The next day when she got home she told her mother that they had "smooth" pancakes for breakfast. "They put in water and poured it out of a bowl!"

When I was little, we ate mostly white bread until the early-mid 1970s, when our aunt got us started using whole grains. After several years of eating whole grain bread, one of my sisters was given a piece of soft, white, store-bought bread. We all crowded around and marveled at the pure whiteness and soft, smooth texture of the bread. We each got a taste until it was gone. But we quickly agreed that we had no desire to go back to white bread. All five of us have been making whole grain bread ever since.

So here is the collection of my favorite whole grain recipes. I've indicated which flours to use with each recipe to get the best results. Using the right flours makes such a big difference in the outcome when you're working with whole grains. And I want you to have success making this delicious goodness for yourselves.

Life for me is such an adventure. I'm constantly learning. When I cook and bake, I'm always experimenting and changing recipes as I go. So take this collection of whole grain recipes and think of them as a starting point. Don't miss my tips. I'm just trying to pass along what I've learned since we aren't sharing the same kitchen.

Discover for yourself the great satisfaction of baking whole grain breads, pies, cookies, scones, crackers—the list is almost endless—and sharing them with your family and friends!

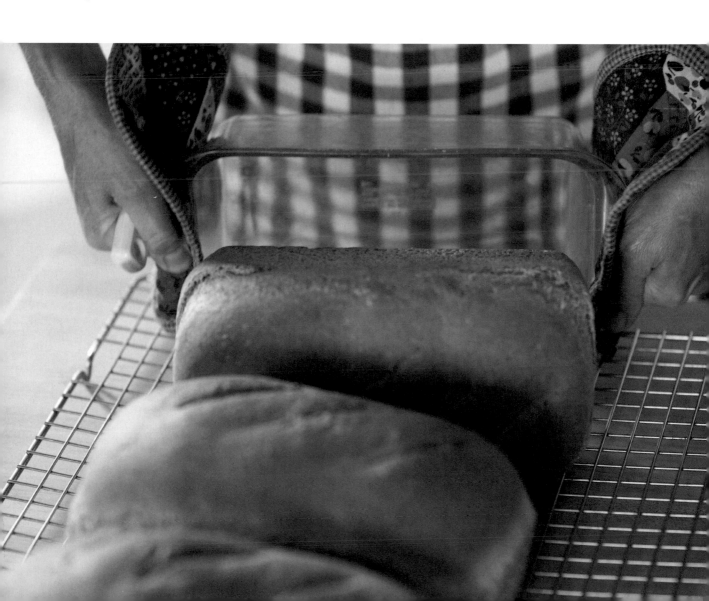

About the Grains Used in This Book

L et me tell you about the grains that I use most often in my everyday baking. Of course many other grains are available, each one containing its own set of nutrients. Experiment with using whatever grains you're drawn to as you become comfortable with whole grain baking.

The simple rustic appearance, full flavor, and grainy feel of whole grains is something that you grow to appreciate. Baking with non-enriched, whole grain flours never produces a smooth, light, super-high loft outcome that is characteristic of all-white-flour baked goods. Be patient with those who need a little time to learn to enjoy whole grains' taste and texture!

I hope that as you try recipes in this book, you'll become confident about adding whole grains to your own favorite recipes. You can use whole grain flour to make almost any baked goods. You just have to learn which flour will work best—and how much to use. Read my grain descriptions closely, and then use the flour or combination of flours most suitable for what you are making. In most of the recipes in this book I use at least half whole grains, along with some white flour. Use more or less, according to your own personal tastes and preferences.

What I've learned along the way

1. When you want to add whole wheat to your own bread recipe, start by using half whole wheat bread flour, while decreasing the amount of bread flour accordingly.
2. If you are using coarsely ground flour and want elastic dough, add 1 generous Tbsp. "vital wheat gluten" per cup of whole wheat bread flour. If you are using other lower gluten grains, do the same. If you're using more finely ground flour, you don't need to use as much gluten.
3. Begin by making small batches and see what works best for you. You may not feel that it is necessary to add gluten.

What is "whole grain"?

A grain is made up of three parts. The **outer protective bran layer** contains the fiber and some nutrients. The **germ** is the fatty, alive part that sprouts if given the chance. It's loaded with Vitamin E, B vitamins, folic acid, and other nutrients. The **endosperm**, the white part, is mostly starch with some protein (or gluten). Whole grain flours have a lower percentage of starch than white milled flours because they contain bran and germ.

These three parts work together to provide whole nutrition. Many package labels say "whole grain," but the germ has likely been taken out or processed to give the product a longer shelf life. The only way to be sure that grains are truly whole is either to grind your own or to find a mill where you can purchase freshly ground grains (see page xxviii for source). Fresh whole grain flour smells and tastes sweet. If it is at all rancid (or partly spoiled), it will have an off-smell and a bitter taste.

To ensure freshness, buy your flours from a place that has a high turnover on its shelves. Because real whole grain flours contain the germ, which is an unprocessed fat, they become rancid if they're not properly stored. To preserve flavor and nutrition, double-bag whole grain flours and store them in a cool, dry, dark place.

If you don't have a good place to store your whole grain flours, or if you don't use them often, double-bag or jar them in small quantities and store them in the refrigerator or freezer. I suggest small quantities because if the air is humid when you get a bag of flour out repeatedly to use it, the cold flour will quickly take on moisture, causing

it to become flat over time. It will still be usable, but it loses flavor and nutritional value. Be sure to bring cold flour to warm room temperature before using it in yeast-risen recipes.

Home baked goods have a short shelf life, especially if they're made with whole grains, and I'm not talking about how fast they disappear when the children come home! Instead, they don't have the added preservatives of many

commercially produced goods, and they contain the germ, which causes them to spoil more quickly. Internal moisture shortens shelf life, so that cobblers, scones, muffins, quick breads, and other more moist baked goods containing baking powder and baking soda turn dark and mold more quickly than drier baked goods. Store them in a cool place out of the direct sun. For longer-term storage, refrigerate or freeze them.

My grandmother used to tell me that when she was a girl, they would make twenty-five pies each week to feed the family and hired help. By the end of the week they would have to scrape some mold off at spots before serving the pies. But they stayed healthy and lived to be quite old!

About wheat and wheat products—"winter" and "spring" flours

"Winter" and "spring" wheat refers to the time of year when the wheat is planted. Winter wheat is planted in the fall. It sprouts, starts growing, and then goes dormant during the cold winter months. It starts growing again as the soil warms up. It's harvested near the beginning of summer.

Spring wheat is planted in early spring and harvested in late summer or early fall.

"Hard" and "soft" flours

Bread flours are made from hard spring wheat. They can be either hard *red* spring wheat or hard *white* spring wheat. White wheat has more protein (gluten) than red. Of the available wheat flours, hard spring wheat flours have the highest percentage of protein (gluten). "Whole wheat bread flour," or "whole wheat flour," is made from the entire grain of hard spring wheat.

Hard winter wheat yields flours with a moderate percentage of protein (gluten). It's used to make flat breads, some artisan breads, and other breads that don't need as fine a texture.

"Pastry flours" are made from the entire grain of soft winter wheat. They can be made from either "soft red wheat" or "soft white wheat." Flour made from soft wheat has a lower percentage of protein (gluten). Gluten produces the elasticity or stretchiness that is characteristic of finely textured yeast breads. In many of my yeast bread recipes I suggest adding gluten if you're using soft wheat, because more gluten is needed for structure.

Pastry flours produce really tender baked goods. They're used in baked goods when you want crumb that breaks easily and lightly apart, without being stretchy. Pies, crackers, pancakes, waffles, fruit cobblers, and scones should have good crumb. To increase crumb in a recipe, increase the amount of pastry flour (whole grain or milled white) and decrease the amount of hard wheat flour and unbleached flour accordingly.

"Red" and "white" flours

The outer bran layer of "red wheat" is dark reddish-brown in color. Red whole wheat flours yield baked goods with a fuller, more robust flavor, as well as a darker appearance. The original wheat strain, known as "turkey red wheat," is the genetic parent for most hard wheat grown in the United States today. In the mid to late 1800s, it was brought to this country by Mennonite immigrant farmers from Russia.

The outer bran layer of "white wheat" (not to be confused with white flour, in which the bran and germ are removed) is light, almost golden in color. White whole wheat flour yields baked goods with a milder, more delicate flavor, a higher loft, and a much lighter appearance. Many bakers say that it lacks flavor, and I agree!

Forms of whole wheat

"Wheat berries" are wheat kernels in their complete, unmilled form. These are viable seeds which will sprout, given the right conditions. Wheat seeds (berries) keep for many years if they're stored in a dry place.

"Cracked wheat" is "wheat berries" that have been cracked and crushed. No heat process is involved. Nothing is taken out.

"Bulgur wheat" is "wheat berries" that have been steamed or parboiled, and then cut and dried. Some of the wheat bran may be removed in the process. Because bulgur wheat is precooked, it cooks up quickly compared to cracked wheat.

"Graham flour" results from the European method of milling whole grain flour. In this process, the endosperm is milled separately from the bran and germ. These elements are then mixed together, resulting in a sweet, somewhat coarser, whole grain flour. Many people prefer graham flour as a superior baking flour. (See p. xxvi for a source for freshly milled graham flour.) Graham flour is a must for making homemade graham crackers.

The grain that I grind by hand is a more coarse flour. I developed the recipes in this book to work with more coarse ground flours. Many of the whole wheat flours available today are more finely milled. You can use them in these recipes, too. The baked goods will have a finer texture. If you're using finer ground whole grain flour, the crumble factor that coarse flour adds won't be as evident.

The ingredients on flour labels can be quite bewildering. If the label on a bag of "whole wheat bread flour" or "bread flour" lists a number of different wheat flours, it means that a combination of different kinds of wheat were needed to reach the required protein (gluten) percentage. If the label on a bag of "all-purpose flour" says it contains only hard winter wheat, the percentage of protein (gluten) of that particular wheat is the same as all-purpose flour (see below). In less expensive all-purpose flours, the different flours listed can be poor quality wheat that doesn't meet the required protein (gluten) standards for other flours. Commercial whole wheat flours may be enriched.

About milled white flours

White flour contains just the endosperm part of the wheat. The bran and germ have been removed. (This is different from white whole wheat flour.) Milled white flour is made from the endosperm of either red wheat or white wheat.

Milled white commercial flours are usually enriched with a variety of enhancers and additives. Even if a label lists wheat as the only ingredient, the flour may contain additives. Individual state laws regulate the amount and kind of information required on food labels.

"Bread flour," sometimes called "high gluten flour" or "strong flour," consists of just the endosperm of the *hard* spring wheat. It has a higher percentage of protein (gluten).

"Pastry flour" is white flour consisting of just the endosperm of *soft* wheat grains. It has a lower percentage of protein (gluten).

"All-purpose flour," sometimes called "wheat flour," is a half-and-half mixture of just the endosperm of hard wheat and soft wheat. Unless it says otherwise on the label, it is probably enriched and maybe even bleached.

"Unbleached flour" is all-purpose white flour that has been naturally aged over time (with no chemicals used) for better baking quality and lighter color. It may or may not be enriched. When white flour is first milled, it has a natural yellow tint. With exposure to the air, the yellow color turns white over the course of time. But this takes weeks or even months.

"Bleached flour" is enriched all-purpose white flour that has been put through a chemical bleaching process to speed the aging process. This gives the flour improved baking quality and a snow-white color.

"Occident flour" originated in Europe. It's an all-purpose flour which *may* contain a slightly higher gluten content than regular all-purpose flour. It is often enriched. It comes bleached or unbleached. It is just like any other white all-purpose flour.

"Cake flour" is bleached, usually enriched, *soft* wheat flour that has been highly milled, producing a super-fine flour that is more absorbent than regular flour. It is used in fine cake and pastry making.

"Gluten" is the non-water-soluble protein in the endosperm of wheat that becomes elastic the more you knead or stir it. Gluten, a pure protein, is used in Asian cooking and vegan food as a meat substitute. To make gluten, add water to milled white bread flour (or whole wheat bread flour). Stir it and knead it, then thoroughly rinse it with water to get the starch out, leaving behind just the protein.

Powdered gluten (often labeled "vital wheat gluten") can be added into bread dough as needed to yield a smooth, elastic product. It is optional in many of my recipes, especially if you are using commercial, finely ground flour. You *can* add too much gluten, which results in rubbery bread.

When I was growing up, real flavored chewing gum was a special treat. We lived on

a farm, and so at harvest-time we liked to make our own. We would chew a mouthful of freshly harvested wheat until all that was left was "gum." We didn't know that what we were chewing on was gluten!

The abrasiveness of coarsely ground flour causes the gluten strands to be cut when kneading bread. If your bread consistently gets crumbly, even after proper kneading, add in some vital wheat gluten. The optional vital wheat gluten I call for in bread recipes gives the added boost that might be needed to form a stretchy, elastic dough. This is my preference and not a necessity. I suggest an amount in the bread recipes. But if you get satisfactory results without using it, great!

You may be wondering if you need to keep a supply of all of these flours. If you want to do whole grain baking, I recommend that you purchase small amounts of the following: (You can refer back to my descriptions to make sense of this!)

- Whole wheat bread flour (hard whole wheat, higher gluten), either red or white, sometimes labeled "100% whole wheat flour" or just "whole wheat flour."
- Whole wheat pastry flour (soft whole wheat, lower gluten), either red or white.
- Pastry flour (soft white flour, lower gluten).
- Bread flour (hard white flour, higher gluten, "strong flour").
- All-purpose flour (a blend of hard and soft white flour, moderate gluten).

Other grains and flours

"Spelt" is an ancient, highly nutritious grain in the wheat family. It is available as "whole grain spelt flour" or as "spelt flour" (which is just the endosperm of the flour). It has a moderate protein (gluten) content.

Whole grain spelt flour has a full, nutty, more robust flavor than wheat. You can use whole grain spelt flour in place of some or all of the whole wheat flour in a recipe that calls for a hard wheat/soft wheat combination. Be gentle in mixing it together with wet ingredients. The gluten in spelt flour activates much more quickly than the gluten in wheat flour. Try using whole grain spelt flour as part of the whole grain flour in yeast breads. You may want to add in some vital wheat gluten because spelt has less protein (gluten) than whole wheat bread flour.

"Durum Wheat" is the hardest of all the wheats and is used in making pasta.

"Cornmeal" has no naturally occurring gluten. It can be roasted for added flavor. Many brands of cornmeal have the bran and germ removed. These cornmeals make the lightest and fluffiest corn-bread imaginable, but for the best nutrition, choose one that includes the whole grain.

"Multi-grain flour" may or may not be whole grain. Only if each grain listed on the label is preceded by the words "whole grain," can you be assured that it is. Otherwise, you're probably getting just the white part (bran and germ removed) of some or all of the grains.

"Flax" is a seed that is mostly fat, not a grain. Adding it to a recipe is like adding in nuts. Many people use flax in baking for its health benefits. Whether flax benefits humans is debatable. Humans cannot digest flax seed in its whole form but only when it's ground.

Since it is a fat, grind it as you need it, or store it in the freezer if it's pre-ground.

If you like the flavor that flax adds, experiment by using it in place of some of the fat in a recipe. For example, try ¼ cup finely ground flax seed in place of 1 Tbsp. of the fat called for in a recipe. A simple coffee grinder works well to grind flax.

Interestingly, linseed oil (used in wood finishes) is made from processed flax seed oil.

The whole seeds of "oats" which have not been cut or rolled are called "groats." Groats are tightly encased in a hull (chaff). They are steamed to more easily remove them from the hull.

Oat groats that have been steamed are not viable seed. They will not sprout. You can purchase non-steamed oat groats at additional expense.

- "Steel-cut oats" are oat groats that are steamed, hulled, and cut into small pieces.
- "Rolled oats" are oat groats that are steamed, hulled, and rolled.
- "Quick oats" are steel-cut oats that, after being cut, are again rolled. They are finer and thinner than rolled oats.
- "Instant oats" are steel-cut oats that are rolled thinly, partially cooked, dehydrated, and flaked.

Of all oat products, "instant oats" contain the least amount of fiber and nutrition.

To make your own oat flour, put several cups of rolled or quick oats in a blender or food processor. Whirl until the flour is as fine as you like it.

Oats have no naturally occurring gluten.

My thoughts about wheat intolerance and wheat nutrition

Wheat and its related grains are a powerhouse of nutrition and fiber if kept in their simplest forms. There are aspects of modern agriculture and modern methods of milling that I'm uncomfortable with, though I certainly don't think we have to go back to planting, harvesting, and threshing by hand. Would we benefit more if wheat were grown in a more sustainable way? High speed milling changes the chemical makeup of flours. Might that affect the way our bodies process wheat? Could much of the wheat intolerance today be a result of what is being done to the wheat, rather than the wheat itself?

People who have been professionally diagnosed with Celiac disease absolutely must avoid all gluten. Before the Industrial Revolution, farmers weren't always able to get their wheat from the field to the barns without it getting wet and having some of it sprout. Because all the work was done by hand, it took a long time to get the harvest in. Some years, farmers were able to get the harvest into their barns without it getting wet. But if it was a wet year, the wheat would sprout, and some of it might even ferment before it was brought into dry storage. It was used regardless of conditions.

Sprouted grains have increased nutritional value. I keep sprouted grains on hand to add along with other flour in my baked goods. There is evidence that sprouted fermented grain is more easily digested. This may help people with mild wheat allergies.

A few years ago, I decided to sprout my own grain (See instructions on page xxiii). Sometimes I get busy and let the sprouting go too long. But I figure a bit of fermentation is in the natural order of things. If you want to experiment, use sprouted grain flour in your bread along with non-sprouted whole grain flours. Or add whole, well-soaked, and drained sprouted wheat or spelt berries as a way to add crunch without having to own a flour grinder. If you don't like the nutlike texture, chop the sprouted wheat in the food processor or blender before adding it into your dough.

My daughter and I have each found that using mostly sprouted grains produces very sticky yeast bread, both when kneading it and in the final baked loaf. I haven't observed any noticeable effect when I use sprouted grain flour in baked goods that are leavened with baking powder and baking soda.

How to sprout grains and then make flour

You can have multiple jars going in this process, but make sure you have enough drying space for all of them if you plan to dry the sprouted wheat berries to make flour.

1. Fill a glass jar halfway with wheat berries. The jar size determines the amount of grain you sprout; often, you can get large jars free from a local deli.
2. Add water. Stir to wash the wheat berries. Pour off the top water containing any chaff.
3. Drain wheat berries through strainer. Repeat.
4. Refill jar with fresh cold water. Let soak in a cool place for 12 hours.
5. Put the strainer on top of the jar. Flip and drain into the sink. Keep the jar upside down in the strainer (over a bowl or in the sink) for 1–2 hours to drain completely.
6. Turn jar upright. 12–18 hours later, little white sprouts should be poking out the end of each wheat berry. You can let them grow up to ¼″ long, but it's not necessary.
7. At this point, refrigerate the sprouted wheat berries. Cook them in a bit of salted water for breakfast. Eat them out of hand like nuts. To add texture to bread, soak the wheat berries in hot water for up to an hour and drain. Pulse lightly in food processor if you want smaller pieces.

How to dry sprouted wheat berries for making flour

1. Spread the sprouted grains in ¼″ layer on cloth-lined food dryer racks or rimmed baking sheets.
2. Dry in a food dryer at 85–100° for 8–12 hours.
3. Alternatively, use the oven. Place the baking sheet(s) in the oven at lowest possible temperature. Stir. Turn off heat, but leave the oven light on. Turn the oven on again once or twice until the wheat is crunchy and completely dry.
4. Another alternative is to spread a cotton sheet with the sprouted wheat in a dry, hot attic. Check after 12 sunny hours.
5. When wheat berries are dry, jar and store in the pantry. If you're concerned that they are still moist, store in refrigerator or freezer.
6. Grind as needed to make flour.

Basic Equipment Makes Baking Fun

I'm accustomed to doing my cooking and baking by hand. I suggest using hand tools and hand instructions in many of my recipes and tips. Some of my recipes work well using a food processor or electric mixer. But don't use them when you're told to fold and mix gently. Machines overwork the dough/batter at those points.

Here are my favorite tools for baking.

- Large, nonreactive, not-too-deep bowls, made of stainless steel, glass, wood, or pottery. Vollrath brand economy bowls are durable stainless steel and have the right depth and slope for easy mixing and stirring. I recommend having a variety of sizes. Several small 1- to 2-quart bowls, (1) 5-quart bowl for smaller recipes like scones and pancakes, (1)16-quart bowl (for making several loaves of bread).
- Sturdy, long-handled, wooden spoon for stirring bread.
- Wooden spoon with a flat stirring edge for lifting, scraping, and stirring while cooking. I like this when I make pie fillings.
- Bench/Dough Scrapers. I like both a flexible one for scraping dough from the bowl and a rigid stainless steel one for cutting dough and scraping/ lifting. Sonridge carries both kinds.
- Stainless Steel Flat Whisk, sometimes called a "roux whisk." Make sure the wires are flexible and not rigid. I use an 8" and a 12" for larger baking jobs.
- Pastry and pizza dual roller. I use this style exclusively. If you have frustrations rolling out pizza dough, pie crusts, or crackers try a Norpro Deluxe Pastry Pizza Roller.

- Strainers: 10", 6", and a set of mini strainers. I recommend ones whose top and handle are in a straight line and lie flat. They store more compactly, and they don't tip during use. Choose a medium mesh. (Super-fine mesh or multi-mesh strainers can clog and stop the flow of whatever is supposed to pass through.)

    10" single mesh strainer to span the sink for easy drainage. It should have a long handle and a single rest loop on the opposite side. I recommend Wasserstrom.

    6" single mesh as a flour sifter and for many other uses.

    Mini strainers are useful for many small straining jobs.

    I use mini strainers for sifting measured baking soda and spices into the other dry ingredients as I bake. I also use them to drain a jar full of soaked wheat when setting it to sprout. After the wheat has soaked for 12–15 hours, I invert whichever size of the three strainers fits in the opening of my glass jar. I then rest it upside down in the sink until the wheat sprouts. It allows the wheat to drain completely. The Prima 3-piece strainer sifter set works well.

- Widemouthed stainless steel canning funnel. Even if you don't preserve food by canning, this is invaluable for filling regular and widemouthed jars. If you store food in jars, you will use this all the time.

- Parchment paper will save many a batch of cookies and other baked goods from spreading and from sticking to the pan. Handle it with care. After using it, place it on a crumb-free surface, carefully scrape it and wipe it off with a lightly dampened cloth. I reuse mine over and over again. The appearance becomes more rustic with each use!

    If you are using the kind that comes on a roll, first mist it, wipe it with a damp cloth, and then place a dry cloth and a cookie sheet on top of it to prevent curling. It should remain flat. Store used parchment paper flat between cookie sheets, or hang it on a skirt hanger in the pantry.

- Half baking sheets, approximately 13"x 18". The uses are endless. Purchase heavy-duty aluminum rather than nonstick. They will last to be handed down to your children. Look for Vollrath sheet pans.

- You'll want at least one thin cookie sheet that has one, or up to three, perfectly flat edges (but don't use AirBake). Along with using it to bake cookies, it makes a great pizza peel. Or use it wherever you need to slide something from a work surface onto another surface. Choose the kind

Grandma used to use—thin but sturdy aluminum, approximately 1 mm thick.

- OXO Good Grips Stainless Steel Food Scale with Pull-out Display, 11-lb. capacity. This is not a necessity but definitely a plus, because weight is the most accurate form of measurement. Measuring cups can vary from brand to brand. (For the most part, I didn't include weight measurements since most of our kitchens are equipped with measuring cups and spoons rather than scales.)
- Measuring cups and measuring spoons. It's hard to recommend a brand because they vary so much in degrees of accuracy. I recommend a good quality set of stainless steel cups and spoons. Use them exclusively. Don't mix and match brands for measuring when making a recipe. I use Lee Valley stainless measuring cups and their simple set of stainless steel measuring spoons.
- Flexible or glass liquid measures: a 4 cup, a 2 cup, and a 1 cup.
- Flex-it Mini Measuring Cup. Accurately measures in tsp. or Tbsp. measurements up to ¼ cup.
- Stainless Steel Zester with optional holder by Lee Valley.
- Flat, handheld, medium-hole grater. It doesn't have to be expensive. Just make sure the holes aren't tiny or the butter will get caught and won't go through.
- Good quality kitchen shears.
- Every working kitchen should have good quality knives. Test their feel before purchasing:
  1. A French chef knife, whatever length and style feels good to you.
  2. Paring knives. It's good to have at least two. I prefer small bladed ones that are forged so that the tang (an extension of the blade) runs right into the handle.
  3. Serrated bread knife.
  4. 1 or 2 slicing/fillet knives.

Dull knives are a cook's nightmare. Never use sharp knives for any use other than what they are intended for. Never wash knives in the dishwasher or place them in the dish drainer or a drawer with other flatware.

Always wipe them with a damp cloth when you've finished using them and immediately put them in a sheath or in a knife block, blade side up.

This keeps them from dulling as quickly. Keep a cheap "beater knife" or knives on hand for those nonfood jobs!

Secret: I've been using the same rather inexpensive set of Chicago Cutlery knives since we were married in 1982. Handled carefully in the above manner they continue to serve me well.

For my straight blade knives I did invest in a Chef's Choice electric knife sharpener. It is user-friendly, does a great job, and I never have to send my knives out to be sharpened.

This may seem like a long list. But keep in mind that good, basic, long-lasting tools make cooking a pleasure. Most of the things on this list are handy for other cooking uses besides baking.

The more you do your own cooking and baking, the lower your grocery bills, even if you are investing in high-quality, organic ingredients!

Ingredient Specifications

All ingredients should be at room temperature unless specified in the recipe. Unsalted butter is my choice for all my baking.

1. You can control the amount of salt that goes into your baked product.
2. There isn't as much liquid incorporated into unsalted butter. If your recipe calls for ½ cup of fat, you don't want 2 or 3 Tbsp. of it to be milky water.

Table salt (meaning salt that is a fine grind) is used in all my baked goods recipes. Its fineness allows for more even distribution. I prefer finely ground pink salt.

Kosher salt is more potent than table salt. It also doesn't incorporate as evenly as table salt. It's not as big a deal in bread baking as it is in other baked goods where you don't work the batter as much.

The vanilla that I use is Shank's Compound Flavoring of Vanilla Beans. It's a combination of real vanilla beans and imitation vanilla flavor. The price is reasonable, and it produces delicious baked goods. There are many other vanilla flavorings available, both pure and imitation. Each one has its own distinctive flavor. I would caution against using cheap imitation flavoring. The flavor it adds is just that: cheap.

My preference for baking cocoa is Aristocrat unsweetened cocoa powder made by Wilbur Chocolate. It's available online. Use chocolate chips that tell you the percentage of chocolate they contain. I prefer 60 percent or higher. Labels that say "dark chocolate" have a high percentage of sugar. "Semi-sweet" is dark chocolate that has a high percentage of sugar.

About fats and oils: When a recipe calls for oil, feel free to use the oil you prefer. My preference is to use fats in their simplest form: Butter, lard, cold pressed nut oils, extra-virgin olive oil, virgin cold pressed coconut oil.

Keep in mind that the fat you use adds its own unique flavor to the finished product. Based on flavor, fats are not always interchangeable in a recipe.

I'm moving away from using oils extracted with petroleum-based solvents and from GMOs. This is why I don' t use vegetable and canola (rapeseed) oils, for example.

Pure oil is expensive and its shelf life is short. To avoid wasting precious ingredients, store cold pressed oils in the refrigerator or freezer.

Use whole grain cornmeal. Two national brands that are whole grain (includes the germ) are Hodgson Mills and Arrowhead Mills. The best and freshest whole grain cornmeal that I

can buy locally is Brinser's Best milled by Haldeman Mills in Manhcim, PA. It comes packaged in a little brown paper bag. A nice little benefit is that it is labeled GMO-free.

1. **Whole grain cakes aren't fine and light textured.** However, the proportions of pastry flour to bread flour, whether it's whole grain or white flour, can change how much the cake hangs together.

I've discovered that a cake made with all pastry flour gets very crumbly, so now I add bread flour. Its additional protein adds structure to the finished cake. Keep the amounts the same as I suggest in these cake recipes, or change the proportions as you like.

Commercial whole grain flours are often ground fine enough to get a decent loft. If you are grinding your own and it's quite coarse, I suggest that you sift it through a medium mesh strainer. Sprinkle the pieces of coarse bran and germ that stay behind over the bottom of the greased baking pan or throw it into your next batch of granola.

2. **Cakes bake best in lighter, brighter pans. Aluminum is the most desirable.** Whatever your pan, even if it's non-stick, grease and flour the sides and bottom. The batter needs something to grab onto to climb the sides of the pan. Additionally, for layer cakes, line the bottom with parchment paper. You may grease and flour the parchment paper, too. Bake cakes in the recommended size pan.

3. **When a cake is baking, walk carefully around the kitchen.** If your old house is like mine and has spring in the floor, it can shake the cake enough to keep it from rising fully.

4. **At the end of the baking time, open the oven door slowly.** Without moving the cake, lightly touch the center with your finger. If it springs back and is leaving the sides of the pan, the cake is finished. To be sure, carefully poke a toothpick into the center. The toothpick should come out clean. If not, gently close the oven door and give the cake a few more minutes.

5. **I use the cheapest toothpicks available as cake testers.** They work, and I always know where the toothpicks are. A cake tester would get lost in my drawer full of useful utensils!

6. **To add whole wheat flour to an angel food cake or white cake would be a mistake.** Some things you just don't mess with.

7. **Creaming butter, sugar, and eggs creates loft in your baked goods.** Cream by hand using a wooden spoon or use an electric mixer. A stick of butter should bend, not mush, in your hands. Cream the butter and sugar. Cream until the mixture is lighter in texture and color. Add room temperature eggs one at a time. Scrape the bowl and beat after each addition. After beating in the last egg and the flavoring the mixture should be light and fluffy. Too much beating will cause a great rise and fall in the baking process. The flour mixture and liquid get added alternately. Add ⅓ of the flour mixture and half of the liquid, beat just to combine. Scrape around the sides and across the bottom of the bowl. Add ⅓ of flour and remainder of liquid. Beat just to combine. Scrape. Add remainder of flour, beat, scrape, and beat until combined. Fold in nuts, fruit etc. Over beating causes stretchy batter resulting in tough cake with tunnels. Under beating, the cake will crumble apart.

CAKES

Easy Chocolate Cake

MAKES: a 9 × 13" or 9 × 9" cake

PREP. TIME: 15 minutes

BAKING TIME: 30–35 minutes

INGREDIENTS FOR 9 × 13" PAN:

¾ cup whole wheat pastry flour

¾ cup whole wheat bread flour

1½ cups all-purpose flour

½ cup unsweetened cocoa powder

2 cups sugar

2¼ tsp. baking soda

1 tsp. salt

⅔ cup oil

1 Tbsp. vinegar

1 Tbsp. vanilla extract

1 cup water

¾ cup cold black coffee *or* water

INGREDIENTS FOR 9" SQUARE PAN:

½ cup whole wheat pastry flour

½ cup whole wheat bread flour

1 cup all-purpose flour

⅓ cup unsweetened cocoa powder

1⅓ cups sugar

1½ tsp. baking soda

½ tsp. salt, slightly rounded

6–7 Tbsp. oil

2 tsp. vinegar

2 tsp. vanilla extract

⅔ cup water

½ cup coffee *or* water

For richer, dark chocolate flavor, increase the cocoa powder by 2–3 Tbsp.

Tart, homemade applesauce always accompanied chocolate cake for dessert when I was growing up.

1. In a large bowl, stir together the dry ingredients: all flours, cocoa, sugar, baking soda, and salt.

2. Add the wet ingredients over top.

3. Stir with a wire whisk, scraping up from the bottom of the bowl until combined. Whisk a few additional strokes.

4. Pour batter into a greased pan.

5. Bake 30–35 minutes in preheated 350°F oven or until a cake tester inserted comes out clean.

If you have whey on hand from cheese making or straining yogurt, this cake does well using whey in place of the water and/or coffee. Omit the vinegar if you use whey.

Shoofly Cake

MAKES: a 9 × 9" or 7 × 11" cake

PREP. TIME: 20 minutes

BAKING TIME: 25–30 minutes

¾ cup whole wheat pastry flour

¾ cup whole wheat bread flour

1 cup all-purpose flour

1 cup brown sugar, packed

½ cup (1 stick) unsalted butter, room temperature

1½ tsp. baking soda

½ cup King Syrup * molasses, warmed slightly (I use the microwave)

1¼ cups boiling water (boil it first before measuring it)

* *If you don't have King Syrup, use Grandma's Original Baking Molasses or Brer Rabbit Gold label. Be aware that they do have a stronger flavor than King Syrup.*

1. In a large bowl, stir together the flours and brown sugar.
2. Grate and cut (scc page 150) the butter into the flour mixture, then work with your hands until the consistency of cornmeal. Set aside ½ cup for topping.
3. Make a well in the remaining crumbs in the bowl. Put baking soda in the well.
4. Pour boiling water and molasses over all.
5. Whisk together until smooth. Batter will be runny.
6. Pour into a greased and floured 9×9" or 7×11" baking pan. Sprinkle with reserved crumbs.
7. Bake for 25–30 minutes in preheated 350°F oven or until a tester inserted in the middle comes out clean. Serve while still warm with ice cream or applesauce.

This cake is moist and nicely rich. If you want a richer cake, add additional:

¼ cup brown sugar
2 Tbsp. butter
2 Tbsp. molasses.

That's how much I cut back from the original recipe.

For a moister cake, reserve ⅔ cup crumbs in Step 2.

German Raw Apple Cake

MAKES: a 9 × 9" cake

PREP. TIME: 25 minutes

BAKING TIME: 30–40 minutes

½ cup whole wheat bread flour

½ cup whole wheat pastry flour

½ cup all-purpose flour

⅛ tsp. salt

1 tsp. baking powder

1 tsp. baking soda

1¼ tsp. ground cinnamon

⅓ cup (5⅓ Tbsp.) unsalted butter, room temperature

⅓ cup brown sugar, packed

⅔ cup sugar

1 large egg, room temperature

⅔ cup thick buttermilk *or* plain lowfat yogurt

2 cups diced, peeled apple, ¼-½" dice

TOPPING:

2 Tbsp. sugar

¼ cup brown sugar, packed

½ cup chopped, toasted walnuts

¼ tsp. ground cinnamon

1. Stir together the flours, salt, baking powder, baking soda, and cinnamon. Set aside.

2. In a mixing bowl, cream butter for several minutes, stopping to scrape the bowl once or twice. The butter should be light and fluffy.

3. Add the sugars and cream until light and fluffy.

4. Add egg. Beat until fluffy.

5. Scrape bowl to be sure the mixture is uniform and beat again if needed.

6. Stir in the apples until just mixed in.

7. In a small bowl, stir together the topping ingredients.

8. Pour the batter into a greased 9×9" baking pan. Sprinkle with the prepared topping.

9. Bake in preheated 350°F oven for 30–40 minutes or until a tester inserted in the middle comes out clean.

Oatmeal Cake

Double the recipe for a 9 × 13" pan. Bake 5–10 minutes longer.

MAKES: an 8 × 8" cake

PREP. TIME: 25 minutes

BAKING TIME: 30–40 minutes

¾ cup room-temperature water

1 cup quick oats *

¼ cup whole wheat pastry flour

¼ cup whole wheat bread flour

⅓ cup all-purpose flour

1 tsp. baking powder

½ tsp. salt

½ tsp. baking soda

¼ tsp. ground cinnamon

¼ cup (half stick) unsalted butter, room temperature **

½ cup brown sugar, packed

½ cup sugar

1 large egg

½ tsp. vanilla extract

TOPPING:

3 Tbsp. brown sugar

⅔ cup unsweetened flake coconut, *optional*

2 Tbsp. unsalted butter, melted and cooled

2 Tbsp. whole milk

¼ tsp. vanilla extract

¼ cup chopped walnuts *or* pecans, *optional*

* *If all you have is rolled oats, allow them to soak at least ½ hour. The water should be nearly all absorbed. Do not use instant oatmeal for this cake.*

** *If you are using salted butter, reduce the salt to a scant ½ tsp.*

1. Pour water over quick oats in a small bowl. Set aside to soak for at least 5 minutes.

2. Stir together the flours, baking powder, salt, baking soda, and cinnamon. Set aside.

3. In a mixing bowl, beat together the butter and sugars just to the consistency of damp sand, about 2 minutes. Scrape down the sides of the bowl.

4. Add egg and vanilla and beat for 30 seconds, just until combined.

5. Add half the dry ingredients and beat until just combined. Add the other half and beat 1 minute.

6. Stir in the oatmeal mixture until just combined.

7. Pour batter into a greased and floured 8" square baking pan.

8. Bake in preheated 350°F oven for 25–35 minutes or until a tester inserted in the middle comes out clean.

9. While the cake is baking, stir together the topping ingredients.

10. Allow the cake to cool a few minutes when it's done baking. Gently spread the topping evenly over the top.

11. Return the cake to the oven and broil several minutes about 9" from the flame until the topping is toasted and golden brown. Watch closely because it burns quickly!

12. Cool cake on a wire rack.

I always thought I disliked carrot cake until I figured out that it's the cream cheese icing I'm not fond of! My extended family is so divided and the debate is so lively on the topic of what icing to put on carrot cakes that I fear I'll have to make two carrot cakes for them each time: one with buttercream icing and one with cream cheese icing.

Carrot Cake

MAKES: a 9 × 13" cake or 2 round 9" cakes

PREP. TIME: 25 minutes

BAKING TIME: 50–55 minutes

¾ cup whole wheat pastry flour

¾ cup whole wheat bread flour

½ cup all-purpose flour

1¼ tsp. baking soda

¾ tsp. salt

1 tsp. ground cinnamon

2 cups finely grated carrots, evenly filled with no air pockets, but not packed

½ cup drained, crushed pineapple, well-drained before measuring

1 cup chopped, toasted walnuts, *optional*

1 cup raisins, chopped with 2 tsp. flour, *optional*

½ cup unsweetened flake coconut, *optional*

3 large eggs

1¾ cups sugar

2 tsp. vanilla

1 cup oil

1. In a bowl, stir together all flours, baking soda, salt, and cinnamon. Set aside.

2. In another bowl, stir together carrots, pineapple, optional walnuts, optional raisins, and optional coconut.

3. In a large, third bowl, beat eggs with a whisk until whites are thoroughly broken up and mixture is uniform.

4. Add sugar and vanilla to eggs. Beat until sugar is mostly dissolved.

5. Add oil and whisk together thoroughly.

6. Add in the dry ingredients and whisk just until smooth and uniform.

7. Using a spatula or wooden spoon, stir in the fruits and optional nuts until evenly distributed.

8. Pour into a greased and floured 9×13" baking pan. To use 9" round baking pans, grease and flour them and add a round of parchment paper to each one.

9. Bake in preheated 350°F oven for 50–55 minutes for 9×13" pan, and 40–45 minutes for round pans, or until cake tests done in the middle and is just beginning to leave the sides of the pan.

10. Place cake pan(s) on wire racks to cool. After 10 minutes, remove the round cakes from their pans to finish cooling. Cool completely before icing.

Butter Cream Icing

MAKES: enough for one 9 × 13" or one 9" layer cake without icing on the sides

PREP. TIME: 15 minutes

3 cups (¾ lb.) confectioners sugar, *divided*

2 sticks unsalted butter, grated or cut in fine chunks *

¼ tsp. salt

3–4 Tbsp. cold heavy cream, *divided*

¾ tsp. vanilla extract

* *If the butter is too warm, the resulting icing will be grainy. The butter should be barely room temperature.*

  If all you have is salted butter, omit the ⅛ tsp salt.

1. Place half the sugar in a deep bowl. Grate in (see page 150) or add the chunks of butter.

2. Use an electric mixture to mix on low until thoroughly combined.

3. Mix in the salt and 2 Tbsp. milk. Beat well.

4. Add the remaining sugar and just enough milk to get a smooth, spreadable icing.

5. Add the vanilla. Whip, adding a few additional drops of milk as needed.

If you want to ice the sides of the cake, as well as between the layers, use these larger amounts:

½ cup (1 stick) unsalted butter
4 cups confectioners sugar
⅛ tsp. salt, slightly rounded
1 tsp. vanilla extract
4–5 Tbsp. cold whole milk *or* light cream

I often have leftover icing in a little jar in the freezer. Because it's all butter and sugar, it thaws quickly. My son Gavin likes to spread that on while the cake is still a bit warm. It does make it delicious.

Gavin's Mug Cake

MAKES: 1 serving in 1 mug

PREP. TIME: 10 minutes

COOKING TIME: 1–3 minutes, depending on the microwave

3 Tbsp. whole wheat pastry flour

2 Tbsp. unsweetened cocoa powder

3 Tbsp. sugar

pinch salt

1 small egg, lightly beaten

1 Tbsp. water

1 tsp. oil

½–1 tsp. vanilla extract

1. In a bowl, mix flour, cocoa powder, sugar, and salt.

2. In a large ceramic mug, lightly whisk the egg. Add the water, oil, and vanilla, and whisk together.

3. Add wet ingredients to the dry ingredients in the mug and whisk together until just combined.

4. Bake in the microwave 1 minute. Microwaves differ in how fast they are. Start with one minute, then keep checking every 10 seconds until it's done.

5. Dust with confectioners sugar and serve warm or just cooled.

You can use a 5" microwave-safe pie plate instead of a mug.

*W*e always ate strawberry shortcake for a main meal when I was growing up. My mom would make a large sheet cake and slice and lightly sweeten 4 or 5 quarts of strawberries into a large serving bowl. You took a piece of cake, piled it high with strawberries, and poured milk over the top. That was a regular main dish in my family during strawberry season. We didn't eat it any other time of the year.

I was the only one in the family who didn't like strawberry shortcake. I dearly disliked soggy cake. I was allowed to eat the components separately, but I wasn't allowed to eat anything else. If we didn't like what was served, we didn't get special provisions! I now love strawberry shortcake in any way, shape, or form.

Strawberry Shortcake

MAKES: a 9" cake

PREP. TIME: 25 minutes

BAKING TIME: 25–35 minutes

1½ cups whole wheat pastry flour

1 cup bread flour

2 tsp. baking powder

½ tsp. salt

⅔ cup sugar

1 cup milk

2 eggs, beaten

1 tsp. vanilla extract

6 Tbsp. cold unsalted butter, melted

strawberries, sweetened if desired, for serving

cold milk, for serving

or whipped cream and sliced strawberries for serving

1. Mix the flours, baking powder, salt, and sugar.

2. Grate and cut in the butter (see page 150), then work with your hands until the crumbs are the consistency of cornmeal.

3. Whisk together the milk, eggs, and vanilla.

4. Pour over the dry mixture. Stir until just combined.

5. Pour into a greased and floured 9" pan.

6. Bake in preheated 350°F oven for 25–35 minutes or until a toothpick inserted near the center comes out clean.

7. Serve warm or cooled with desired toppings.

Blueberry Buckle

MAKES: a 9" pan or 9 × 13" pan

PREP. TIME: 20 minutes

BAKING TIME: 25–50 minutes

INGREDIENTS FOR 9" SQUARE PAN:

STREUSEL:

⅓–½ cup sugar

⅓ cup whole wheat pastry flour

½–1 tsp. ground cinnamon

¼ cup (half stick) soft butter

CAKE:

¼ cup (half stick) unsalted butter, room temperature

½–⅔ cup sugar

1 large egg

½ tsp. vanilla extract

¾ cup whole wheat pastry flour

¾ cup whole wheat bread flour

½ cup all-purpose flour

2 tsp. baking powder

½ tsp. salt

½ cup milk

2 cups blueberries

extra blueberries for serving, *optional*

INGREDIENTS FOR 9 × 13" PAN:

STREUSEL:

½–¾ cup sugar

½ cup whole wheat pastry flour

¾–1½ tsp. ground cinnamon

6 Tbsp. soft butter

CAKE:

6 Tbsp. unsalted butter, room temperature

¾–1 cup sugar

2 large eggs

¾ tsp. vanilla extract

1¼ cups whole wheat pastry flour

1 cup whole wheat bread flour

¾ cup all-purpose flour

1 Tbsp. baking powder

¾ tsp. salt

¾ cup milk

3 cups blueberries

extra blueberries for serving, *optional*

If you're using frozen blueberries, they can be starting to thaw but shouldn't be juicy. Fold them into the batter. Pour the batter into the prepared pan and allow to set 15–20 minutes before baking. This allows the blueberries to thaw and keeps them from discoloring the batter. It will take longer to bake.

1. Make the streusel topping by stirring together sugar, flour, and cinnamon in a bowl. Work in the soft butter until soft crumbs; it is important that the butter is not melted. Set aside.

2. Separately, stir together all flours, baking powder, and salt. Set aside.

3. In a mixing bowl, cream butter for several minutes until it is light and fluffy.

4. Add sugar. Cream together, stopping to scrape the bowl once or twice to make sure the mixture is uniform.

5. Add in the egg(s). Beat until fluffy.

6. Add a third of the flour mixture and half the milk to the butter mixture. Beat until just combined.

7. Scrape down the sides of the bowl. Repeat with another third of flour and the rest of the milk. End with the last third of the flour and beat until thoroughly combined.

8. Gently fold the blueberries into the cake batter.

9. Pour the cake batter into a greased and floured baking pan. Sprinkle streusel evenly over the batter.

10. Bake in preheated 375°F oven for 25–30 minutes for the 9" pan and 40–50 minutes for 9×13" pan or until a toothpick inserted comes out clean. If you notice the cake is getting too browned before it is finished, you may want to reduce the temperature to 350°F.

11. Serve warm topped with extra blueberries.

Cherry Squares

MAKES: 35 squares

PREP. TIME: 20 minutes

BAKING TIME: 35–40 minutes

¾ cup (1½ sticks) unsalted butter, room temperature

1¼ cups sugar

4 large eggs

1 tsp. vanilla extract

¼ tsp. almond extract

½ cup whole wheat pastry flour

½ cup whole wheat bread flour

1 cup all-purpose flour

1 tsp. baking powder

½ tsp. salt

2¼–2½ cups cherry pie filling *

* *See cherry pie filling on page 117. Increase the thickener by 2 Tbsp. when making the filling for these bars.*

   If you don't have access to cherries for making your own pie filling, purchase a good quality can of cherry pie filling and doctor it by adding ⅛ tsp. salt, 1 Tbsp. melted butter, and ¼ tsp. almond extract.

1. In a large bowl cream butter and sugar until light and fluffy.

2. Add eggs one at a time, beating after each addition. Scrape the bowl to make sure the creamed mixture is uniform. Add the vanilla and almond extracts. Beat again.

3. Separately, stir together flours, baking powder, and salt. Add to butter mixture and mix until flour is totally incorporated and batter is uniform.

4. Pour batter into greased and floured 13×18" jelly roll pan or half sheet pan.

5. Using a table knife, score the batter with 5 lines lengthwise and 7 lines crosswise, to yield roughly 48 2¼" squares.

6. Dollop 1 Tbsp. of the cooled pie filling into the center of each square.

7. Bake in preheated 350°F oven 35–40 minutes or until the cake springs back when touched. The cake will bake up around the little crater of pie filling.

8. Cool. Cut into squares. If you wish, dust with powdered sugar for pretty just before serving.

For hurry-up Cherry Squares, don't score the dough. Just dollop the pie filling at intervals on the dough. It's still attractive!

You can halve this recipe and bake it in a 9×13 pan.

1. **Cobblers and crisps tend to be versatile, so you can often choose a different fruit than the one called for in the recipe.** You may need to adjust the amount of sugar you use, depending on the natural sweetness or ripeness of the fruit you choose.

2. **If you're using a 9 × 9 baking dish, don't use more than 3 cups of fruit, or you risk having the cobbler or crisp bake over in your oven.**

3. **When using frozen fruit, allow it to thaw just a bit.** The cobbler or crisp will take longer to bake due to the cold internal temperature.

4. **If you have leftovers, the flavors may actually improve overnight.**

5. **Cobblers and crisps can keep several days at room temperature.** They also freeze well for future use.

6. **Cobblers and crisps are not only wonderful desserts.** They are also satisfying breakfasts or even a supper if you've had a main meal mid-day.

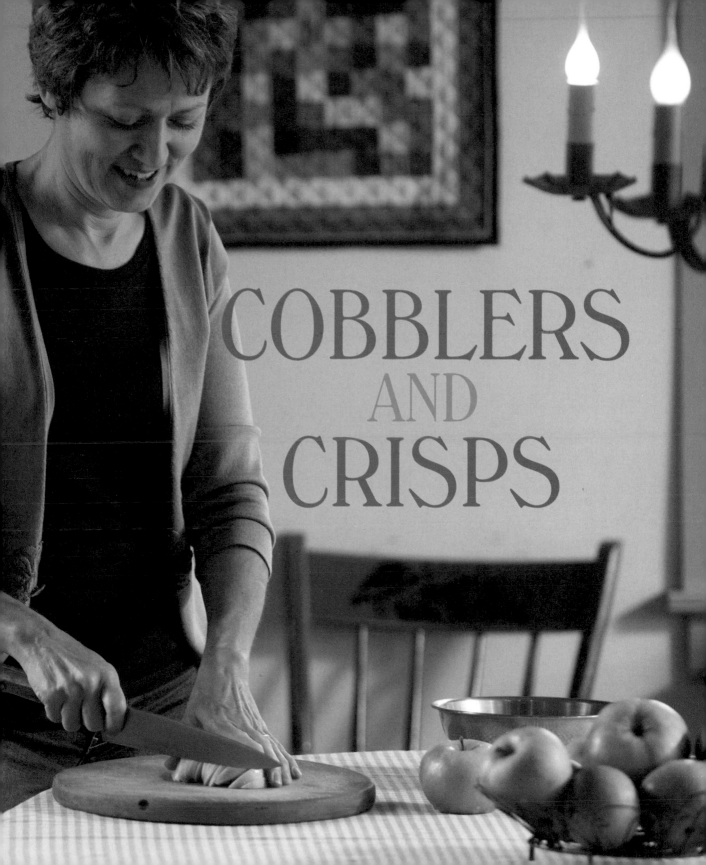

COBBLERS AND CRISPS

Hearty Apple Crisp

MAKES: a 9 × 13" pan

PREP. TIME: 20 minutes

BAKING TIME: 20–35 minutes

5–6 cups peeled, sliced, tart baking apples (I like a combination of apples)

²/₃–³/₄ cup cane sugar, brown sugar, or maple sugar

1 tsp. ground cinnamon

¼ tsp. salt

1 Tbsp. lemon juice if you don't have tart apples, *optional*

3½ cups rolled *or* quick oats

²/₃–1 cup cane sugar, brown sugar, or maple syrup

¼ tsp. salt

12–14 Tbsp. butter, melted

1. In a large bowl stir together the apple slices, sugar, cinnamon, salt, and optional lemon juice.

2. Spread in a 9×13" baking pan.

3. In the same large bowl, stir together the oats, sugar, and salt.

4. Add the melted butter and stir together until thoroughly combined.

5. Sprinkle oatmeal topping evenly over the pan of apples.

6. Bake in preheated 375°F oven for 20–35 minutes, until topping is golden and the apples in the center of the pan are soft when pierced with a toothpick. Baking time depends on how small the apple pieces are and how soft you like your baked apples.

7. Enjoy warm or cold with milk or ice cream.

Fruit Crumble

MAKES: a 9 × 13" pan

PREP. TIME: 20 minutes

BAKING TIME: 25–35 minutes

4½–5 cups any combination of blueberries, blackberries, red *or* black raspberries, strawberries, peaches, etc.

¼–1 cup sugar, depending on the sweetness of the fruit *

¼ tsp. salt

2 cups whole wheat pastry flour or whole grain spelt flour

2 cups rolled *or* quick oats

1½ cups brown sugar, packed

1 tsp. ground cinnamon

pinch ground nutmeg, *optional*

1 cup (2 sticks) cold, unsalted butter

* *The amount of sugar is to taste. It does lose the special dessert quality the more you cut back.*

1. In a bowl, stir together the fruits, sugar, and salt. Set aside.

2. In a large bowl, stir together the flour, oats, brown sugar, cinnamon, and optional nutmeg.

3. Grate the cold butter into flour mixture (see page 150). Use a flat whisk or pastry blender to work further until you have fine crumbs.

4. Lightly press half of the crumbs into the bottom of a greased 9×13" glass baking pan.

5. Add the berry mixture and spread evenly over the pressed crumbs. Sprinkle the remaining crumbs over the berries.

6. Bake in preheated 350°F oven for 25–35 minutes or until bubbly and golden. Cool slightly and serve warm with milk, ice cream, or whipped cream.

> *You can use frozen fruit. Thaw slightly, stir in the sugar, and assemble the Crumble. After the Crumble is assembled, allow fruit to thaw a while longer to cut down on the baking time.*

Rhubarb Strawberry Crunch

MAKES: a 9 × 13" pan

PREP. TIME: 20 minutes

COOKING TIME: 5–10 minutes

BAKING TIME: 35–45 minutes

2 cups whole wheat pastry
flour (you may use part
whole grain spelt flour)

1 cup quick *or* rolled oats

1 cup brown sugar, packed

½ tsp. salt

⅔ cup cold, unsalted butter

1 cup sugar

2 Tbsp. Clear Jel (not instant)
or cornstarch

¼ tsp. salt

1 cup water

4 cups diced rhubarb, fresh
or frozen

1 cup fresh *or* frozen whole
small strawberries, halved
if they're large

1 Tbsp. frozen orange juice
concentrate, *optional*

*To make Rhubarb
Crunch, replace the
strawberries with
1 cup additional
rhubarb.*

1. In a large bowl, stir together flour, oats, brown sugar, and salt.

2. Grate (see page 150), cut, and work in the butter until the consistency of cornmeal.

3. Sprinkle—do not press—half of the crumbs evenly over the bottom of a greased glass 9×13" baking dish.

4. In a heavy-bottom pan, stir together the sugar, Clear Jel, and salt. Add the water and stir again.

5. Stir in the rhubarb. Using a flat-edge wooden spoon or spatula, cook and stir gently so as not to break up the rhubarb. Cook until boiling and thickened.

6. Remove from the heat. Stir in the strawberries and optional orange juice concentrate.

7. Carefully pour fruit mixture evenly over the crumbs in the baking pan.

8. Sprinkle the remaining crumbs over the top.

9. Bake in preheated 350°F oven for 35–45 minutes or longer until bubbly around the edges and golden on top. You may serve it hot, but we found that it tastes best the next day.

I serve this fruit cobbler hot with milk as a delicious Saturday evening meal, and then leftovers cold for breakfast on Sunday morning.

Fruit Cobbler

MAKES: a 9" pan

PREP. TIME: 15 minutes

BAKING TIME: 10–20 minutes

CHERRY

3 cups fresh *or* frozen sour *or* Montmorency cherries *

½–¾ cup sugar

pinch salt

2 tsp. quick-cooking tapioca

¼ cup water

BLACK RASPBERRY

3 cups fresh *or* frozen black raspberries **

¼–½ cup sugar

pinch salt

2 tsp. quick-cooking tapioca

¼ cup water

PEACH & RED RASPBERRY

2 cups fresh *or* frozen peaches *

1 cup fresh *or* frozen red raspberries **

¼–½ cup sugar

2 tsp. quick-cooking tapioca

pinch salt

1 tsp. fresh lemon juice

2–3 Tbsp. water

The kinds of fruit and amounts of sugar are to personal taste. You may use any one fruit or combination that you like. To enhance the flavors of mild fruits add in 1–2 teaspoons of fresh lemon juice and a pinch of salt. Unless your baking dish has extra deep sides, do not exceed 3 cups of fruit for a 9" square pan.

PEACH

3 cups fresh *or* frozen peaches

⅓–½ cup sugar

2 tsp. quick-cooking tapioca

pinch salt

2 tsp. fresh lemon juice

2–3 Tbsp. water

dash ground cinnamon

BATTER

1¼ cups whole wheat pastry flour

¼ cup pastry flour

2 tsp. baking powder

¼ tsp. salt

6 Tbsp. cold, unsalted butter

1 large egg, beaten

⅓ cup milk

¼ cup sugar

* *I freeze pitted sour cherries with the sugar on them. They marinate in the sugar and are ready to be used straight from the freezer. See recipe introduction on page 117 for more details.*

** *Black raspberries should be frozen unwashed and unsweetened. Washing red or black raspberries toughens the skins during the freezing process.*

NOTE: *A drop or two of almond extract added to the cherry or peach cobbler adds an interesting dimension.*

1. Spread chosen fruit(s) over the bottom of a 9" square pan. Sprinkle with the other fruit sauce ingredients that accompany your chosen fruit. Stir.

2. Cover loosely and place in cold oven. Preheat oven to 375°F. The fruit heats while the oven heats. It needs to be hot and bubbly before adding the cake topping (about 15 minutes). Stir once or twice.

3. In a large bowl whisk together the flours, baking powder, and salt.

4. Grate cold butter on top of dry ingredients (see page 150). Fluff with a fork. Use a flat wire whisk or pastry blender to cut it in until the butter is nearly all incorporated.

5. Separately, beat together the egg, milk, and sugar.

6. Pour the liquid mixture over the dry ingredients. Stir until the mixture just comes together.

7. Remove the bubbling hot fruit from the oven. Stir.

8. Drop dollops of dough evenly on top. If your fruit was hot enough, it will start to bake before you get it back in the oven. Don't worry if they're not evenly spaced. They will bake together.

9. Return the cobbler to the oven and watch it closely because it will get done quickly, in 10–20 minutes.

To make a 9 × 13 pan, make 1½ batches (up to 5 cups fruit).

I've developed these recipes to be lower in sugar and fat. If you wish for a richer dessert, increase the sugar in the fruit and dot 1–2 Tbsp. butter over the hot fruit just before topping with the dough. Increase the sugar in the dough to ¾ cup.

Granola

MAKES: about 15 cups*

PREP. TIME: 20 minutes

BAKING TIME: 2 hours

10 cups rolled *or* quick oats

1¼ cups sugar, more *or* less to taste

3 cups whole grain spelt flour *or* whole wheat pastry flour

1 cup chopped walnuts *or* pecans

1 cup sliced almonds

¼ cup pecan meal

1–1½ tsp. salt, to taste

1 cup oil of your choice *or* melted fat

1 cup water

* *You can halve or double this recipe.*

1. In a large bowl stir together the dry ingredients. Add the fat and water and stir until thoroughly combined.

2. Spread on 2 rimmed baking sheets.

3. Bake in preheated 300°F oven for 2 hours, stirring every 30 minutes. The chunks should be completely dry.

4. Cool. Place in quart Mason jars or other airtight containers.

Because of all the nut oils and the fact that there aren't any preservatives, this will get stale more quickly than factory-made granola. Vacuum-seal it in jars, or bag and freeze what you aren't going to use within a week.

Experiment with fats for added depth of flavor:
—Virgin expeller pressed oil, melted.
—Butter, melted.
—Walnut or other nut oils add a lot of flavor.

Optional additions:

1–2 tsp. ground cinnamon

1–2 cups chopped pecans *or* walnuts

¼ cup ground flax

grated coconut

Replace the water with 1 cup pure maple syrup. Reduce the sugar by ¼–½ cup.

Stir in dried fruit after the granola is baked and cooled.

½ cup ground toasted pumpkin seeds *(I save the seeds that I scoop out of butternut squash. Wash, drain, and spread them on a baking sheet to dry in a warm oven. Grind them in a coffee grinder or blender.)*

1. **You can add whole grains to many of your favorite cookie or bar recipes.** I mostly make recipes that hide the whole grains. People who aren't used to whole grains don't know the difference. I suggest that you start out with half whole grains, using part whole wheat pastry flour and part whole wheat bread flour, along with all-purpose flour. Increase the whole grain flour in small increments with successive batches. Decrease the all-purpose flour accordingly.

If your home-ground whole wheat flour is coarse and grainy, cut back on the liquid by 1–2 Tbsp. for every cup of liquid called for in the recipe. If the recipe doesn't call for any liquid, increase the whole grain flours by 1 or 2 Tbsp. for every cup of flour called for in the recipe. The bran and germ, which make up about 17 percent of the flour, aren't as absorbent as all-white flour.

2. **Cookies bake more consistently on parchment and can quickly be removed from the baking sheet.** This is especially helpful if you arc baking multiple batches and don't have multiple baking sheets. Simply slide the paper containing the cookies onto your cooling surface. Handled carefully, parchment is reusable time and time again. Just brush off the crumbs.

Store the sheets flat between your baking sheets. The "baked on" look of the parchment paper doesn't affect your next baked goods. Parchment-lined baking sheets are slippery when filled with cookies. To prevent your cookies from sliding, keep the pan level as you place it in the oven.

3. **For soft chewy cookies:** Take the cookies out of the oven when they're slightly underbaked. Underbaked cookies are set up and slightly golden at the edges. Their middles are just slightly gooey. (Completely gooey isn't done enough.) They continue to bake and get firmer as they sit on the hot baking sheets. Let them rest for up to 2 minutes before sliding them onto a wire rack. If they're already the right chewiness when taken from the oven, skip the resting time and slide immediately from the pans.

4. **Cake-type cookies should spring back when you touch their middles,** unless you're aiming for a crispy, hard cookie. Remove these from the baking sheets immediately to a wire rack to cool.

5. **If you have problems with your cookies spreading too much:**
   - Chill your dough before baking.
   - Make a note to add 1 or 2 Tbsp. additional flour to your dough the next time.
   - Always use parchment paper on your baking sheet.
   - Your oven may be slow, not actually reaching the temperature you set it to. Increase the temperature by 25°.

6. **You can substitute other whole grains tablespoon for tablespoon, but be careful of strong flavors.** A cookie should taste like a cookie and have the texture of a cookie, not a biscuit. Otherwise, you can turn people off to the world of whole grains.

7. **Make extra cookies to have on hand in the freezer.**

8. **I prefer not to change the flour in cake-y cookies such as sugar cookies. They can look gray and unappealing.**

9. **As long as your mixing bowl is big enough, you can double or halve any cookie recipe.**

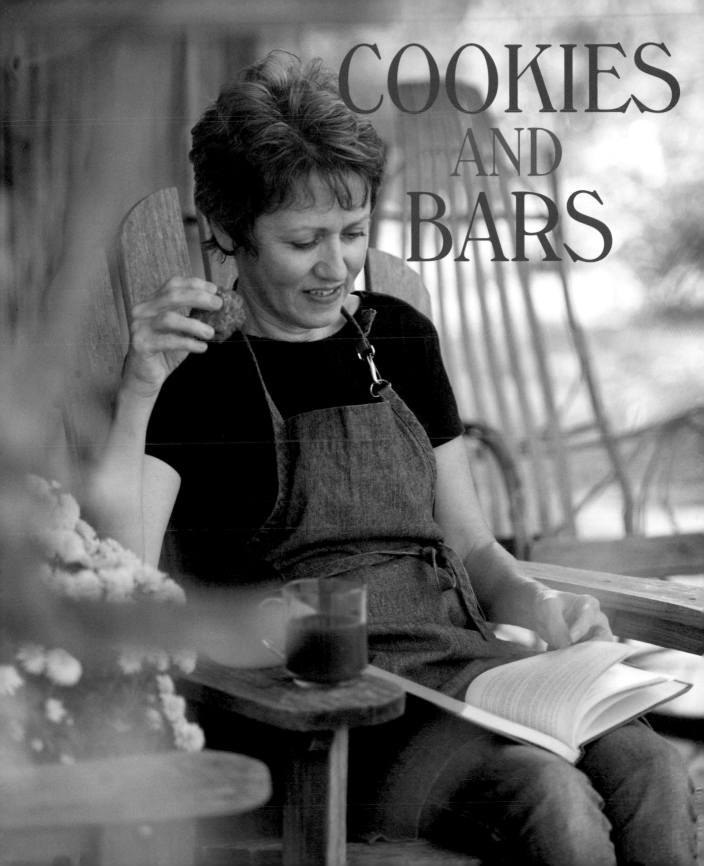

COOKIES
AND
BARS

Chewy Chocolate Cookies

MAKES: 2 dozen cookies

PREP. TIME: 20 minutes

BAKING TIME: 8–12 minutes

½ cup (1 stick) unsalted butter

1⅓ cups sugar

⅔ cup brown sugar

⅔ cup plain lowfat yogurt or ½ cup Greek yogurt filled to ⅔ cup with milk

2 tsp. vanilla extract

¾ cup whole wheat pastry flour

½ cup whole wheat bread flour

¾ cup all-purpose flour

½ tsp. baking soda

½ tsp. salt

½ tsp. baking powder

¾ cup unsweetened cocoa powder

1 cup chocolate chips

½–¾ cup toasted almonds *or* walnuts

1. Melt butter. Pour into a mixing bowl.

2. Stir in sugars until combined.

3. Stir in yogurt and vanilla.

4. In a separate bowl, mix together flours, baking soda, salt, baking powder, and cocoa powder. Stir them into the butter mixture until combined.

5. Stir in chocolate chips and nuts.

6. Drop by tablespoon 2" apart on parchment-lined baking sheets.

7. Bake in preheated 350°F oven for 8–12 minutes, or until edges are set and the middle is slightly gooey.

8. Allow hot cookies to cool 2 minutes on the pans. Remove to wire racks to cool.

Molasses Crinkles

MAKES: about 3 dozen cookies

PREP. TIME: 20 minutes

CHILLING TIME: 1–2 hours

BAKING TIME: 8–10 minutes

¾ cup (1½ sticks) unsalted butter, room temperature

1 cup brown sugar, packed

1 large egg, room temperature

¼ cup full-flavor molasses (Brer Rabbit green label or Grandma's original molasses)*

2¼ cups whole wheat pastry flour

2 tsp. baking soda

1 tsp. ground cinnamon

1 tsp. ground ginger

½ tsp. ground cloves

¼ tsp. salt

sugar, for rolling the balls of dough

The best molasses for these cookies is a full-flavored baking molasses. Blackstrap molasses is too bitter.

1. In a large bowl, cream the butter and brown sugar.

2. Add the egg and molasses and beat until fluffy.

3. In a small bowl, mix the flour, baking soda, spices, and salt.

4. Add half the dry ingredients to the butter mixture. Mix.

5. Add the rest of the dry ingredients and mix until well combined.

6. You can chill the dough for 1–2 hours at this point.

7. Roll dough into 1" balls. Dip the top of each ball into sugar.

8. Place each dough ball on parchment-lined baking sheets.

9. Bake for 8–10 minutes in preheated 375°F oven, or until edges are set and middles are slightly underbaked.

10. Allow hot cookies to sit on the baking sheets for 2 minutes.

11. Remove from baking sheets and cool completely on wire rack before storing in an airtight container.

If you don't have time to chill the dough and roll the balls, you can just drop the cookies from a teaspoon and sprinkle sugar on top. Still delicious!

Chocolate Peanut Butter Sandwich Cookies

MAKES: 18 sandwich cookies

PREP. TIME: 30 minutes

CHILLING TIME: 8–12 hours

BAKING TIME: 10 minutes

COOLING TIME: 20–30 minutes

CHOCOLATE COOKIES:

9 Tbsp. (1 stick + 1 Tbsp.) unsalted butter

½ cup unsweetened cocoa powder

¼ cup chocolate syrup

2 Tbsp. natural peanut butter

1 large egg, room temperature

1 cup brown sugar, packed

1 tsp. vanilla extract

¾ cup whole wheat pastry flour

½ cup whole wheat bread flour

¾ tsp. baking soda

pinch salt

PEANUT BUTTER FILLING:

2 Tbsp. unsalted butter, room temperature

¼ cup natural peanut butter

¼ cup milk

½ tsp. vanilla extract

2¾ cups powdered sugar

1. To make the cookies, melt butter over low heat.

2. Stir in cocoa powder, chocolate syrup, and peanut butter until smooth. Cool.

3. In a large mixing bowl, beat the egg and brown sugar until smooth.

4. Add the chocolate mixture. Add vanilla. Beat again.

5. In a separate bowl, combine flours, baking soda, and salt.

6. Add about half of the flour mixture to the chocolate batter. Stir. Add the rest of the flour mixture and stir again until just combined.

7. Cover the bowl of dough tightly. Chill overnight for 8–12 hours.

8. When ready to bake cookies, drop dough by level tablespoons onto parchment paper-lined cookie sheets.

9. Bake in preheated 350°F oven for 10 minutes or until just set in the middle.

10. Cool on pan 2 minutes before removing to rack to cool completely.

11. Make the Peanut Butter Filling. In a medium bowl, beat butter and peanut butter until smooth.

12. Add milk and vanilla. Gradually beat in powdered sugar until the filling is smooth and a bit fluffy.

13. Spread the peanut butter filling on the bottom of one cookie and top with a second to make a delicious little sandwich. Repeat with remaining cookies and filling.

Chocolate Chip Oatmeal Cookies

MAKES: 3 dozen cookies

PREP. TIME: 25 minutes

BAKING TIME: 10–13 minutes

COOLING TIME: 2 minutes

½ cup (1 stick) unsalted butter, room temperature

½ cup brown sugar, packed

½ cup sugar

1 large egg, room temperature

½ tsp. vanilla extract

1 cup rolled oats

½ cup whole wheat pastry flour

½ cup whole wheat bread flour

½ tsp. baking powder

½ tsp. baking soda

½ tsp. salt

½ cup unsweetened cocoa powder

6 oz. Ghirardelli 60%-cacao chocolate chips

¾ cup chopped walnuts *or* pecans, toasted lightly for extra flavor

1. In a mixing bowl, cream together butter and sugars.

2. Beat in egg and vanilla.

3. Place rolled oats in blender or food processor. Grind until powdery. Now you have oat flour.

4. In another mixing bowl, mix oat flour, both whole wheat flours, baking powder, baking soda, salt, and cocoa powder.

5. Stir flour mixture into butter mixture by hand. The dough will be stiff.

6. Add chocolate chips and nuts. Stir again—the dough is very stiff!

7. Use a cookie scoop to make 1 Tbsp. balls. Place on a parchment-lined baking sheet.

8. Bake in preheated 350°F oven for 10–13 minutes, until edges are set up and middle is slightly gooey.

9. Allow cookies to sit on the baking sheets for 2 minutes before removing to a wire rack to finish cooling.

These cookies are quite rich with chocolate. If you prefer a milder chocolate flavor, omit the dark chocolate powder, or grate a 6-oz. milk chocolate bar on a microplane grater and stir that in.

Peanut Butter Cookies

MAKES: about 3 dozen

PREP. TIME: 20 minutes

BAKING TIME: 8–10 minutes

½ cup (1 stick) unsalted butter, room temperature

½ cup natural peanut butter

⅓ cup sugar

⅓ cup brown sugar, packed

1 tsp. vanilla extract

1 large egg, room temperature

¾ cup whole wheat pastry flour

½ cup all-purpose flour

1 tsp. baking soda

¼ tsp. salt

sugar, for dipping

1. In a mixing bowl, cream the butter, peanut butter, and sugars until smooth.

2. Beat in vanilla and egg until fluffy.

3. Separately, combine flours, baking soda, and salt.

4. Add flour mixture to creamed mixture. Stir until flour is just combined.

5. Roll dough into 1″ balls.

6. Dip tops in sugar if you wish, or press criss-cross with a fork.

7. Place sugary dough balls 2″ apart on parchment paper-lined baking sheets.

8. Bake in preheated 375°F oven for 8–10 minutes or until edges are set up and middles are slightly gooey.

9. Allow cookies to sit on baking sheets for 2 minutes before removing to wire racks to finish cooling.

To make Peanut Blossoms: As soon as the cookies are removed from the oven, press an unwrapped chocolate kiss firmly into the middle of each cookie. Remove cookies from sheets and cool until the chocolate sets.

Soft Oatmeal Raisin Cookies

This dough can be made ahead and chilled.

MAKES: 3–3½ dozen cookies

PREP. TIME: 20 minutes

CHILLING TIME: 8–24 hours

STANDING TIME: 1 hour

BAKING TIME: 10–12 minutes

2 large eggs

¾ cup raisins

½ cup whole wheat pastry flour

¼ cup whole wheat bread flour

½ cup all-purpose flour

¼ tsp. salt

½ tsp. ground cinnamon

1 tsp. baking soda

1 cup rolled oats

½ cup chopped pecans or walnuts, *optional*

½ cup (1 stick) unsalted butter, room temperature

⅓ cup brown sugar, packed

½ cup sugar

1 tsp. vanilla extract

Raisin cookies are a great way to use up raisins that dried out and became a bit crystallized. The raisins soak up the egg and you never know the difference.

1. In a small bowl or pint jar, whisk the eggs. Add in the raisins and stir. Cover.

2. Chill this mixture at least 8 hours and up to 24 hours. The raisins will absorb a lot of the eggs. Allow to stand at room temperature 1 hour before proceeding to make the cookies.

3. In a bowl, combine the flours, salt, cinnamon, baking soda, oats, and optional nuts. Set aside.

4. In a mixing bowl, cream butter and sugars until light and fluffy.

5. Add vanilla and soaked egg/raisin mixture. Cream until thoroughly combined. Some of the soft raisins may break up.

6. Add the dry ingredient mixture and mix by hand until well incorporated.

7. Drop by tablespoons 2" apart onto parchment-lined baking sheets. Now turn on the oven to preheat. Let cookies rest while the oven preheats.

8. Bake in preheated 350°F oven for 10–12 minutes or until they are set in the middle when pressed with your finger. These are a cake-type cookie. The centers shouldn't be at all gooey.

9. Slide onto a wire rack to cool completely.

These are truly soft raisin cookies. I've made many different raisin cookie recipes over the years. Many recipes become dry after a day or two. These stay soft because the raisins are thoroughly soaked, so they don't continue to leach moisture out of the baked cookie.

This is a very old family recipe (not the whole wheat part—I added that) handed down through the generations of my sister-in-law's Amish family. They kept a tin of these crispy cookies on hand at all times during the winter. To soften a cookie, they would lay it on the hot wood stove before dunking it into hot chocolate or milk fresh from the family cow.

Old-Fashioned Ginger Snaps

MAKES: 4½ dozen large cookies

PREP. TIME: 20 minutes

CHILLING TIME: 3–4 hours

BAKING TIME: 12–15 minutes

¾ cup lard (no substitutions!)

¾ cup sugar

1 cup full-flavored (Brer Rabbit green label) molasses

1–2 Tbsp. ground ginger, depending on how much gingery zip you like

1 Tbsp. ground cinnamon

1 Tbsp. baking soda

¼ cup boiling water (measure after boiled)

1½ cups whole wheat pastry flour

1½ + ⅓ cups all-purpose flour

sugar, for sprinkling, *optional*

1. In a large bowl, cream the lard and sugar until fluffy.

2. Add in molasses, ginger, cinnamon, and baking soda.

3. Pour boiling water over the lard mixture. Stir. The purpose of the hot water is to dissolve the baking soda.

4. Combine flours.

5. Add flours to molasses mixture. Stir by wooden spoon, or, the old-fashioned method, with your bare hands. The dough will be very stiff.

6. Cover bowl. Chill well for 3–4 hours.

7. Roll out a hunk of dough on a floured board to ½" thick and no thinner. Rolled any thinner, the cookies won't crackle.

8. Cut 2" rounds right up next to each other to get the maximum amount of cookies from your rolled dough. The more you roll the dough, the more flour gets incorporated into it, and the drier the cookies become.

9. Place cookies 2" apart on parchment-lined baking sheets. Sprinkle with optional sugar if you wish. Repeat with remaining dough.

10. Bake in preheated 325°F oven for 12–15 minutes. The puffiness must be going down before removing the cookies from the oven.

11. Slide onto wire racks to cool completely. If the cooled cookies are crispy, they will keep for months stored in a tin at a cool room temperature (not next to a heat source!).

My sister-in-law remembers how her mother cleaned out the molasses jar when she was making these cookies. She would turn the bottle upside down to get out the last pourable molasses, then swish hot water through the jar to get the very last bit of sweetness out. She would then use that hot water/molasses mix as the hot water in these Ginger Snaps.

Monster Cookies

MAKES: 6–7 dozen cookies

PREP. TIME: 25 minutes

STANDING TIME: 1 hour

BAKING TIME: 8–12 minutes

4 large eggs, room temperature

⅔ cup unsalted butter (1 stick + 2½ Tbsp.), room temperature

2 cups salted peanut butter

2 cups brown sugar, packed

1 cup sugar

1 tsp. vanilla extract

½ tsp. salt ✳

2½ tsp. baking soda

5 cups rolled or quick oats

1 cup whole wheat pastry flour, or whole grain spelt flour

⅔ cup chocolate chips

⅔ cup coarsely chopped peanuts or M&Ms

✳ If using unsalted peanut butter increase the salt to 1 tsp.

1. In a large bowl, beat together eggs, butter, peanut butter, brown sugar, sugar, vanilla, and salt.

2. Stir in baking soda, oats, flour, chocolate chips, and peanuts or M&Ms.

3. Allow dough to sit for 1 hour for oats to absorb moisture.

4. Drop by tablespoonsful onto parchment-lined baking sheets.

5. Bake in preheated 350°F oven for 8–12 minutes until edges are set up and middles are just slightly gooey.

6. Allow cookies to sit on baking sheets for 2 minutes. Transfer to wire rack to finish cooling.

Oatmeal Date Bars

MAKES: a 9" pan

PREP. TIME: 20 minutes

BAKING/COOKING TIME: 50–55 minutes

1 pound chopped, pitted dates (a scant 3 cups)

2 Tbsp. + ½ cup sugar, *divided*

½ cup water

1 cup whole wheat pastry flour

2 cups rolled *or* quick oats

½ tsp. baking soda

¼ tsp. salt

½ cup (one stick) cold, unsalted butter

1. Place the dates, 2 Tbsp. sugar, and water in a small saucepan. Simmer uncovered until soft. Mash with a fork and set aside.

2. In a large bowl, mix flour, oats, baking soda, ½ cup sugar, and salt.

3. Grate the cold butter on top of the flour mixture (see page 150).

4. Use a pastry cutter or flat whisk to cut in the butter to form crumbs.

5. Press ⅔ of the crumb mixture into the bottom of a greased 9" baking dish.

6. Spread date mixture on top.

7. Sprinkle remaining crumbs on top and lightly press down.

8. Bake in preheated 350°F oven for 40–45 minutes or until golden. Cool on wire rack before cutting into bars.

Chocolate Chip Bar Cookies

These are thick, chewy chocolate chip cookies made in bar form.

MAKES: a 9 × 13" pan of bars

PREP. TIME: 20 minutes

BAKING TIME: 20–30 minutes

COOLING TIME: 20 minutes

2 cups + 2 Tbsp. whole wheat pastry flour

2 Tbsp. flax meal, *optional*

½ tsp. baking soda

½ tsp. salt

¾ cup (1½ sticks) melted unsalted butter, cooled

½ cup brown sugar, packed

½ cup sugar

1 large egg, room temperature

1 egg yolk, room temperature

2 tsp. vanilla extract

10 oz. chocolate chips, any sweetness level you like

1 cup chopped, toasted pecans

1. Mix flour, flax meal, baking soda, and salt. Set aside.

2. In a large bowl, whisk the butter, sugars, eggs, and vanilla.

3. Fold in the dry ingredients.

4. Stir in the chocolate chips and nuts.

5. Spread batter into a greased 9 × 13" baking pan.

6. Bake in preheated 325°F oven 20–30 minutes. To get soft chewy bars, you need to underbake them. The center of the pan should be just set, not runny. The outer edge will be completely set, but still soft. The surface will have a very thin, shiny crust.

7. Cool at least 20 minutes before cutting into bars.

Molasses Raisin Strips

MAKES: 2 dozen

PREP. TIME: 25 minutes

BAKING TIME: 15–18 minutes

½–¾ cup raisins *
½ cup all-purpose flour,
   divided
1 cup whole wheat pastry
   flour
¼ cup whole wheat bread
   flour
1 tsp. baking powder
½ tsp. baking soda
¼ tsp. salt
½ tsp. ground cinnamon
dash ground allspice
½ cup (1 stick) unsalted
   butter, room temperature
¼ cup white sugar
¼ cup brown sugar, packed
1 large egg
¼ cup Brer Rabbit mild
   (gold label) molasses,
   or Grandma's Original

* *If you're not fond of raisins,
you can eliminate them or
chop them so fine that you
don't know they're there.*

*For a fancy touch,
make a thin glaze
and drizzle it
diagonally over the
logs before cutting
them into strips.*

1. In a mixing bowl, mix the raisins with 2 tsp. of flour taken from the ½ cup. Chop floured raisins to desired size.

2. Separately, combine the whole wheat flours, the rest of the flour, baking powder, baking soda, salt, cinnamon, and allspice. Whisk to combine.

3. Stir the chopped raisins and any remaining flour from the chopping surface into the dry ingredients. Set aside.

4. In a mixing bowl, cream butter and both sugars until smooth.

5. Add the egg. Beat well until mixture is uniform.

6. Add molasses. Beat well, stopping to scrape the bowl and check that the batter is uniform.

7. Add dry ingredients to the creamed mixture along with the raisins. Beat until just combined.

8. Line a large baking sheet with parchment paper. Divide the dough into three equal portions.

9. Shape each piece of dough into a log 2×8". Place on the parchment with space between to allow spreading during baking.

10. Bake in preheated 375°F oven for 12 to 16 minutes, until the center of the logs springs back when touched lightly.

11. Cool logs on pan for 2 minutes. Slide the parchment with the logs on it to a wire rack to cool completely.

12. Cut each log into 8 strips.

13. Remove to a wire rack to cool completely. Store in an airtight container.

Granola Bars

MAKES: 24 bars

PREP. TIME: 20 minutes

BAKING TIME: 30–50 minutes

CHERRY ALMOND

1 cup sliced almonds

1 cup quick oats

2 cups quick *or* rolled oats

¼ cup whole wheat pastry flour

1 cup finely chopped dried cherries, *or*
  more if desired

½ tsp. salt

2 large eggs

½ cup brown sugar, packed

½–¾ cup sugar

¼ cup oil *or* melted, cooled unsalted butter

½ tsp. vanilla

¼–½ tsp. almond extract

¼ cup water

PEANUT RAISIN

1 cup finely chopped peanuts

1 cup quick oats

2 cups quick *or* rolled oats

2 Tbsp. whole wheat pastry flour

2 Tbsp. whole wheat bread flour

1 cup finely chopped raisins, *or* more if desired

½ tsp. salt

2 large eggs

½ cup brown sugar, packed

½ cup sugar

¼ cup honey

¾ cup natural unsalted peanut butter

1 tsp. vanilla extract

¼ cup water

If the dried fruit is sticking to your knife too much to chop easily, use a little of the measured flour from the recipe to sprinkle on them and chop. Pick up the flour with the blade of your knife and toss it over the chopped raisins as needed. When finished, use a bench scraper to pick up the fruit and all remaining flour.

ORANGE CRANBERRY NUT

1 cup sliced almonds *or* pecan pieces

2 cups quick *or* rolled oats

1 cup oat flour

⅓ cup whole wheat pastry flour

¼ tsp. salt

1½ cups chopped dried cranberries

1 large egg

½ cup sugar

¼–½ cup brown sugar, packed

5 Tbsp. unsalted butter, melted and cooled

1 Tbsp. orange juice concentrate

2 Tbsp. milk

½ tsp. orange zest, *optional*

½ tsp. vanilla extract

DATE PECAN BARS

*Use chopped **dates** and **pecans** in place of cranberries and almonds in **Orange Cranberry Nut** granola bars. Omit the orange juice concentrate and orange zest. Add **3 Tbsp. milk** and **¼–½ tsp. cinnamon**.*

1. Spread nuts and the first amount of quick oats in baking pan. Toast at 325°F for 10–20 minutes or until lightly golden. Stir occasionally. Set aside to cool.

2. Place second amount of oats in food processor or blender and pulse to make coarse flour. The texture should be a little coarser than flour with little pieces of oats throughout.

3. Pour oat flour in mixing bowl. Stir in remaining dry ingredients and chopped dried fruit.

4. In another bowl whisk the egg(s) well.

5. Stir rest of ingredients into the beaten egg.

6. Pour the wet ingredients over the dry ingredients and stir to combine.

7. With well-buttered hands, spread and firmly press the mixture into a greased 9×13" pan.

8. Use a sharp knife or pizza cutter to cut into 24 bars (or the size you want).

9. Bake in preheated 350°F oven for 20–30 minutes or until lightly golden.

10. Cool and wrap individually or store in an airtight container. The flavor of these improves if left to set for a day.

You can use any dried fruit or a combination of fruits in this recipe. The finer you chop the fruit, the better the bars hold together.

To make these bars gluten-free, omit whole wheat flour. Use gluten-free oat flour or flour of your choice.

Cherry Almond Granola Bars

Peanut Raisin Granola Bars

Orange Cranberry Nut Granola Bars

1. **Making crackers is a little bit like making pie crust**. Roll it out once. If you are having trouble with the dough sticking to your board, roll out smaller amounts at a time. The only difference is you'll have more edge pieces. Feed the baked edge pieces to the children, or mix them in with the perfect ones so that people see that they're homemade. Home-baked crackers will be the talk of the party!

2. Some recipes tell you to roll the crackers directly on a baking sheet. But **if you roll them out on another surface, they bake much more evenly and don't stick to the pan.** After you've rolled them out, place the unbaked crackers a tiny bit apart on parchment-lined baking sheets.

3. **If some of the thicker/bigger crackers seem a bit soft or flexible** after they have cooled 5–10 minutes, put them back onto the warm baking sheet and return to the still quite warm oven to crisp them up. They can stay in there until the oven cools completely if need be.

4. **I store crackers in a parchment-lined tin in a warm, dry place** (behind the wood stove is perfect). They will keep for up to 2 weeks like this, but freeze them if you don't plan to use them soon, or if you don't have a warm, dry place to store them.

   To refresh crackers, remove the lid and place the tin directly into a warm oven, or place the crackers on a baking sheet. Let them set in a warm oven until crispy.

5. **Just a suggestion: refrain from eating the whole batch of crackers in one sitting!** They're loaded with salt and fat. It's my opinion that the right amount (plenty!) of salt is key to making good crackers.

6. **You can easily double or halve any of the cracker recipes.**

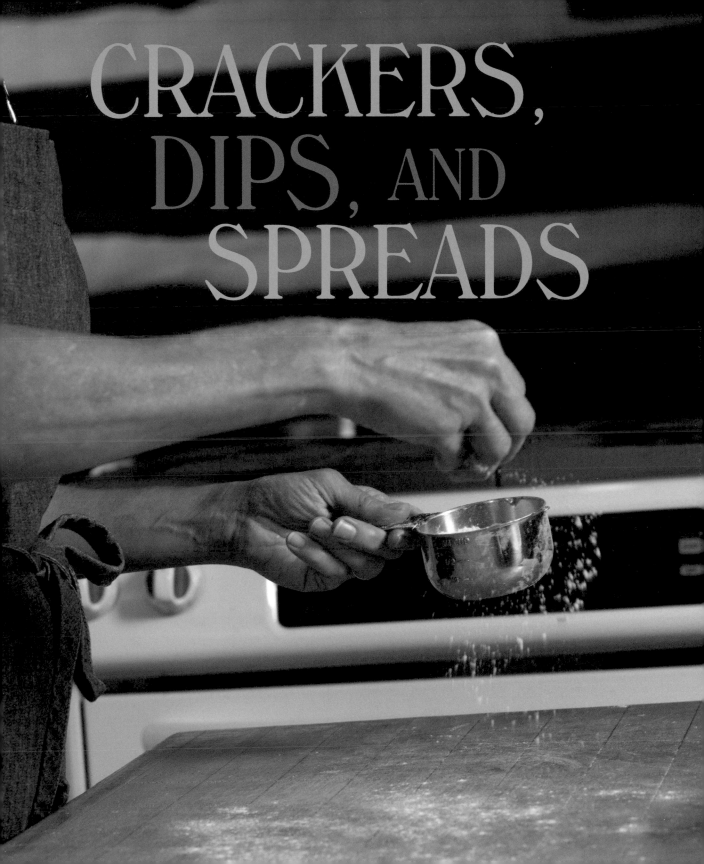

CRACKERS, DIPS, AND SPREADS

Wheat Crackers

MAKES: 8 ounces

PREP. TIME: 30 minutes

BAKING TIME: 5–8 minutes

1¼ cups whole wheat pastry
    flour

1 Tbsp. sugar

½ tsp. salt

¼ tsp. baking powder

½ tsp. paprika

4 Tbsp. (half stick) cold,
    unsalted butter

3½–4 Tbsp. milk

⅛ tsp. vanilla extract,
    optional

salt, for sprinkling, *optional*

1. In bowl, combine the dry ingredients.
2. Grate, toss, and cut in the butter (see page 150). Work with your fingers to make coarse crumbs.
3. Stir in the milk, using the lesser amount, and optional vanilla.
4. Roll dough to ⅛" thickness on floured surface.
5. Sprinkle with additional salt and/or optional seasonings. Roll lightly to adhere seasonings.
6. Prick all over with a toothpick or sharp-tined fork.
7. Cut into 1–1½" squares using a pizza cutter.
8. Place squares on parchment lined baking sheet.
9. Bake in preheated 375°F oven for 5–8 minutes, switching racks at 3 minutes for even baking. Look for golden, crispy crackers at 5 minutes. Remove those, and put any underbaked crackers back in the oven for 1–3 minutes, checking and removing when they are golden and crispy.
10. Slide parchment with crackers onto rack. Cool.

Flavor variations to add in Step 5:

¼ tsp. granulated
    garlic
finely chopped fresh
    or dried herbs
¼ tsp. fresh ground
    black pepper
seasoning salt or
    other flavored
    salts

a Toasted Cracker
ONE POUND NET

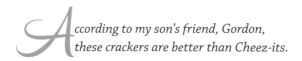

According to my son's friend, Gordon, these crackers are better than Cheez-its.

Cheese Crackers

MAKES: 12 ounces

PREP. TIME: 30 minutes

BAKING TIME: 7–10 minutes

1⅓ cups whole wheat pastry flour

⅔ cup unbleached pastry flour

1 tsp. salt

¼ tsp. white pepper

¼ tsp. dry mustard powder

⅛ tsp. cayenne, *optional* to give them kick

½ cup (1 stick) cold, unsalted butter

2 ounces (a generous ¾ cup) finely grated sharp cheese—mostly extra-sharp cheddar, but a little Asiago or Parmesan is good, too

6–7 Tbsp. cold milk

salt, for sprinkling, *optional*

1. In large bowl, stir together flours, salt, pepper, mustard powder, and optional cayenne.

2. Grate in the cold butter (see page 150) and cheeses. Toss with a fork.

3. Use a flat whisk or work with fingers until the mixture has the texture of coarse meal.

4. Using a sharp-tined fork, stir in the cold milk, using the lesser amount, until the mixture comes together in a ball. Add the other tablespoon of milk if there are too many crumbs not sticking into the ball.

5. Divide dough in half.

6. Flour your work surface and roll dough to ⅛" thick.

7. Lightly sprinkle with more salt if you wish. Roll or pat the salt into the surface.

8. Prick all over with a toothpick. Use a pizza cutter to cut into small squares.

9. Place on parchment-lined baking sheets.

10. Bake in preheated 375°F oven for 7–10 minutes, switching racks at 4 minutes for even baking. Look for golden, crispy crackers at 7 minutes. Remove those, and put any underbaked crackers back in the oven for 1–3 minutes, checking and removing when they are golden and crispy.

11. Slide onto cooling racks to cool.

Don't use soft cheeses such as mozzarella or American cheese. They will gum up and won't work in nicely. Plus, they won't add the flavor that's needed to make a tasty cheese cracker.

Black Pepper Oat Crackers

Eat fresh avocado scooped right out of the shell with the crackers. Very nutritious lunch or snack.

MAKES: 8–9 ounces

PREP. TIME: 30 minutes

BAKING TIME: 7–10 minutes

2 cups rolled oats

3 Tbsp. whole wheat pastry flour

3 Tbsp. unbleached pastry flour

1 Tbsp. sugar

¾ tsp. baking powder

1½ tsp. salt

½–1 tsp. fresh ground black pepper, depending on how peppery you like things

¼ cup (half stick) cold, unsalted butter

6 Tbsp. cold milk

salt, for sprinkling, *optional*

1. Place measured oats into bowl of food processor or blender. Pulse until you make coarse flour.

2. In large bowl, combine the oat flour, wheat flours, sugar, baking powder, salt and black pepper.

3. Grate in the cold butter (see page 150) and cut in with flat whisk or work in with fingers until it's the texture of coarse meal.

4. Stir in the cold milk until mixture comes together in a ball.

5. Divide dough in half. Roll on floured board to ⅛" thick.

6. Sprinkle with additional salt if desired. Roll lightly to press the salt into the crackers.

7. Use a pizza cutter to cut into desired size crackers.

8. Place on parchment-lined baking sheets.

9. Bake in preheated 375°F oven for 7–10 minutes, switching racks at 4 minutes for even baking. Look for golden, crispy crackers at 7 minutes. Remove those, and put any underbaked crackers back in the oven for 1–3 minutes, checking and removing when they are golden and crispy.

10. Slide onto cooling racks to cool.

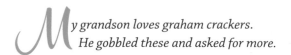

My grandson loves graham crackers.
He gobbled these and asked for more.

*To make cinnamon grahams, add ½ tsp. cinnamon to dough. Sprinkle rolled dough with cinnamon sugar and roll again lightly before cutting.

Honey Graham Crackers

MAKES: 16 standard size graham crackers

PREP. TIME: 45 minutes

BAKING TIME: 10–15 minutes

1 ½ cups graham pastry flour

⅓ cup pastry flour

½ tsp. baking powder

¼ tsp. baking soda

¼ tsp. salt

¼ cup sugar

6 Tbsp. cold butter

1 Tbsp. + 1 tsp. whole milk

2 Tbsp. honey

1 tsp. vanilla extract

1. In a large bowl, stir together the dry ingredients.

2. Grate (see page 150) and cut the cold butter into the dry ingredients. Cut it in with a flat whisk or 2 table knives. Then use your fingers to work until the consistency of damp sand.

3. In a separate bowl stir together 1 Tbsp. milk, 2 Tbsp. honey, and 1 tsp. vanilla.

4. Pour milk mixture over flour mixture. Stir until it comes together into chunks. Cut through the chunks and roll them around to pick up the crumbs. Add a few drops of the 1 tsp. milk as needed to get the remaining crumbs to stick to the stiff dough.

5. Divide dough evenly in half. Cover with plastic wrap and refrigerate while you prepare your paper. You may stop and chill the dough at any point in the following process.

6. Cut 3 pieces of parchment paper at least 13″ × 15″. If you want perfect graham crackers, mark a 9″ × 10 ½″ rectangle on one of the pieces.*

7. Break one of the chilled balls of dough into small pieces and place them at even intervals within the marked rectangle.

8. Place an unmarked piece of parchment paper on top and press down to flatten the pieces of dough. Use a Pastry and Pizza Dual Roller to roll the dough within the marked rectangle. There will be empty spots.

9. Peel off the top paper. Some dough will stick; don't worry about that now. Use a pizza cutter or offset spatula to trim up the dough edges to match the drawn rectangle. Fill the empty spots with the trimmings.

10. Cover with the parchment paper and roll the dough to an even ⅛" thickness. Flip the sandwiched dough and roll the other side to even out any wrinkles. Repeat rolling, trimming and filling holes if needed.

11. Make sure the marked paper side is up. Peel back and remove the marked paper. Scrape off any dough that stuck. Smooth back onto the dough surface. Square up the edges.

12. Using a pizza cutter or blunt knife, cut the dough lengthwise down the center. Make 3 evenly spaced widthwise cuts to yield 8 rectangles. Score (but do not cut the whole way through) these rectangles in half lengthwise and widthwise to yield 4 rectangles in each cracker.

13. Use the blunt end of a skewer or a fork to poke holes in each scored section.

14. Place the unmarked parchment containing the prepared crackers on a baking sheet and set aside. Repeat Steps 7–13 with the other half of the dough.

15. Bake both trays in preheated 350° **F** oven for 10–15 minutes, switching racks as needed for even baking. Crackers should be golden around the edges and firmly set in the middles. Once again, run the pizza cutter through the cut lines. Slide the parchment containing the crackers onto a cooling rack.

16. Break apart and store in an airtight container for up to 2 weeks. Or freeze for future use. The flavor of these crackers improves over the next days.

The crackers will become more crispy when cooled. If they aren't crispy, they were either rolled too thick or underbaked. Place crackers back into the still-warm oven to dry out.

If perfect graham crackers aren't important to you, roll the dough ¹/₈" thick but ignore the rectangle and perfect cutting process. Cut as you wish, poke holes, and bake as instructed.

Bonus Baking Tips!

1. When using parchment paper on cookie sheets, keep the baking pan level at all times. If you tilt it as you are putting it into the oven the parchment containing your goods will slide.

2. Oven baking times vary. My daughter and I have the extremes. Depending on what she's baking, her oven takes up to15 minutes more time than mine.

3. Sift lumpy baking soda, baking cocoa, and spices through a small mesh strainer into dry ingredients.

4. Artificial and low calorie sweeteners used in place of sugar don't caramelize during baking. They produce dry, dull baked goods. Use sparingly or not at all.

5. In many of my recipes I have you stir the sugar into the liquid ingredients. That's because sugar is actually a liquid. Stir through the combined liquids, making sure to get all the sugar up from the bottom before adding it to the dry ingredients.

6. To melt butter for use in a recipe, put the desired amount in a small saucepan or microwavable bowl. Melt halfway. Remove from heat and stir until melted. You have melted, cooled butter.

7. To grease a pan, I take a bit of butter on my fingertips and give the pan a good coating on the bottom and up the sides. A light coating is all that's needed unless a recipe calls for well greased, then be generous and don't miss any spots. Greasing a pan in this way is messier than spray, but there are no chemicals, no container to throw away, and you get a bit of skin softening in the deal. Or keep a 1" natural bristle brush in a tall narrow spice jar with a bit of oil in the bottom. To grease a pan, use the oiled brush. It takes up minimal space in the cupboard where it's ready to grab and use. Every once in a while, when it's empty, brush out the oil and wash the container and the brush.

Sesame Thins

MAKES: 8 ounces

PREP. TIME: 30 minutes

BAKING TIME: 5–8 minutes

¾ cup whole wheat pastry flour

¼ cup pastry flour

½ tsp. salt

½ cup sesame seeds, toasted and cooled, *divided* *

½ tsp. baking powder

4 Tbsp. (half stick) cold, unsalted butter

1 tsp. low-sodium soy sauce

3–4 Tbsp. cold milk

salt, for sprinkling, *optional*

* *Toasting the sesame seeds is optional.*

1. Combine both flours, salt, ⅓ cup sesame seeds, and baking powder.

2. Grate (see page 150), toss and cut in the butter. Work in a bit with your hands to make coarse crumbs.

3. Stir in soy sauce and the lesser amount of milk until the dough comes together in a ball.

4. Roll dough to ⅛" thickness on floured board.

5. Sprinkle with remaining sesame seeds and optional salt. Roll lightly to adhere the seasonings.

6. Use a pizza cutter to cut into desired size crackers.

7. Place on parchment-lined baking sheets.

8. Bake in preheated 375°F oven for 5–8 minutes, switching racks at 3 minutes for even baking. Look for golden, crispy crackers at 5 minutes. Remove those, and put any underbaked crackers back in the oven for 1–3 minutes, checking and removing when they are golden and crispy.

9. Slide onto cooling rack to cool completely.

Layered Pesto Torte

MAKES: a 10" pan, cut into wedges

PREP. TIME: 45 minutes

CHILLING TIME: several hours up to several days

CHEESE SPREAD:

16 oz. cream cheese, room temperature

½ cup (1 stick) unsalted butter, room temperature

1 cup whole-milk ricotta

¼ tsp. salt

BASIL PESTO:

½ cup sliced almonds or walnuts or pine nuts

2 cloves garlic, coarsely chopped

130 grams basil leaves (roughly 3 cups lightly packed, piled up)

30 grams (approximately ½ cup) fresh grated Parmesan cheese

Pinch fresh lemon zest

3–4 tsp. fresh lemon juice

½ cup extra-virgin olive oil

1–2 tsp. kosher salt, to taste

3 Tbsp. room temperature butter

TOMATO PESTO:

½ cup sliced almonds or chopped walnuts

1 clove garlic, coarsely chopped

2 cups coarsely chopped sun-dried tomatoes

½ cup freshly grated Parmesan cheese

½ tsp. salt

½–¾ cup extra-virgin olive oil

1. Beat together the ingredients of the cheese spread until evenly combined. Cover. Chill.

2. In the bowl of a food processor, add all the ingredients for the basil pesto. Pulse until evenly smooth.

3. Remove pesto to a covered container. Chill.

4. In the same food processor bowl (no need to wash it), add all the tomato pesto ingredients. Pulse until smooth.

5. Remove tomato pesto to a covered container and chill.

6. Prepare the springform pan to mold the layerd dip. Place a large square of parchment paper or plastic wrap on the detached bottom of a 9" or 10" springform pan.

7. Clamp the sides around the lined pan. Fold the extra paper or plastic up around the outside of the pan. This is to catch any ooze as you layer the dip.

8. Spread ⅓ of the cheese mixture evenly over the bottom of the lined springform pan.

9. Place it on a baking sheet in the freezer for at least 30 minutes. Can freeze up to a day before proceeding.

10. Now you will make the rest of the layers, freezing the dip each time for 30 minutes–24 hours before adding a new layer.

11. These are the layers that go over the initial third of the cheese mixture from Step 8: all of the basil pesto, another third of the cheese mixture, all of the tomato pesto, the final third of the cheese mixture. Cover and freeze.

This layered dip seems like a lot of work, but remember that you are making dip to have on hand for many get-togethers to come. You can break the steps up over several days. You can freeze both pestos ahead of time, and the cheese mixture can be made up to two days ahead of time.

12. To portion the dip into wedges before storing for future occasions, allow the dip to thaw a little in the refrigerator until it is possible to cut it with a sharp knife.

13. Cut layered dip into desired size wedges. Wrap each wedge tightly in plastic wrap, and double-bag to ensure freshness. Freeze.

14. To serve, unwrap the frozen wedge entirely and place it on a plate. Cover lightly and thaw for several hours or overnight in the refrigerator.

15. Serve with crackers or vegetable sticks for a nutritious, delicious snack. You're certain to be asked for the recipe!

Use basil pesto as a spread on whole grain bread, pizza, omelets, or pasta, etc. I make many batches in the summertime when basil is plentiful. Freeze it in small jars. It freezes and thaws and re-freezes beautifully.

Yogurt Dill Dip

MAKES: 1½ cups

PREP. TIME: 10 minutes

CHILLING TIME: several hours

1½ cups plain not nonfat Greek yogurt *or* part sour cream

¼ tsp. dry mustard

½ tsp. salt

1 tsp. paprika

1 clove garlic, minced *or* ¼ tsp. granulated garlic

1 tsp. whole dill seed, crushed *or* 2 tsp. chopped fresh dill weed

1 Tbsp. minced onion

1 Tbsp. minced fresh parsley

1 Tbsp. minced fresh chives

1. Whisk all together in a bowl.
2. Cover. Chill several hours to blend flavors. Serve with raw vegetables for dipping.

To make as a salad dressing, use plain not nonfat yogurt in place of Greek yogurt. Add 1 Tbsp. fresh lemon juice or vinegar.

You may use dried parsley and chives (1 tsp. each), but pass on using the dried minced onion with its tough, chewy little pieces.

Black Bean Salsa

MAKES: about 4 cups

PREP. TIME: 15 minutes

CHILLING TIME: 3–4 hours

2 cups cooked, drained
black beans

1 cup frozen whole kernel
corn, thawed and
drained

3–4 plum tomatoes,
seeded and chopped

¼ cup chopped green
onion

1 clove garlic minced
or ¼ tsp. granulated
garlic

2 Tbsp. chopped fresh
parsley *or* 2 tsp. dried

2 Tbsp. fresh lemon juice

2 Tbsp. extra-virgin olive
oil

1 tsp. chili powder

½ tsp. ground cumin

¼ tsp. dried oregano

¼–½ tsp. salt, according
to your taste

1. Mix all together in a large bowl. Cover.

2. Chill at least 3 or 4 hours. Serve as a dip with tortilla chips or homemade crackers, or on top of scrambled eggs for breakfast.

1. When making muffin batter, it's better to leave a few streaks of dry ingredients than to over-mix it. The batter will continue to get mixed as you fill the pans. Over-mixing causes tough muffins with tunnels streaked throughout.

You don't need fancy electrical equipment to make muffins and quick breads. In fact, it is easier to be accurate when mixing by hand. Stand mixers and food processors tend to over-mix.

2. When using frozen fruit, allow it to thaw just a bit. Toss the not-mushy frozen fruit into the dry ingredients mixture. Add wet ingredients and carefully mix until barely stirred together. Fill the muffin pans and let them sit while the oven preheats. **They will take longer to bake due to the cold internal temperature.**

3. Adding more fruit than called for in the recipe causes the fruit to sink to the bottom of the muffins.

4. Don't bother using paper liners if you are going to eat the muffins fresh. Paper liners stick to the freshly baked muffin, peeling away the outer layer. Why throw away good food? Instead, dip a pastry brush in oil or soft butter and thoroughly grease the bottoms and up the sides of your muffin tins. A light dusting of flour after greasing them is even better. Fill. Bake. Cool slightly, then run a thin-bladed knife around each muffin. They should pop right out.

5. Muffin pans are simple to wash if you soak them right away. Do not use detergent, as that takes away the seasoning. Quickly twirl a stiff round brush around in each soaked muffin cup. Rinse. Put in the still-warm oven to dry.

MUFFINS

Cranberry Pecan Muffins

MAKES: 12–15 muffins

PREP. TIME: 30 minutes

BAKING TIME: 15–25 minutes

1¾ cups pecan halves

2 cups fresh *or* frozen cranberries, thawed slightly

4 tsp. confectioners sugar

¼ tsp. salt

STREUSEL TOPPING:

3 Tbsp. whole wheat pastry flour

2 Tbsp. sugar

2 Tbsp. unsalted butter

pinch salt

2 large eggs, room temperature

¾ cup sugar

½ cup milk, room temperature

½ cup whole wheat pastry flour

½ cup whole wheat bread flour

1½ tsp. baking powder

½ tsp. salt

⅓ cup unsalted butter, melted, cooled

1. Spread pecan halves on a rimmed baking sheet. Bake at 325°F, stirring often, until lightly toasted. Put toasted pecans in a bowl and set aside to cool completely.

2. Coarsely chop the fresh or partially frozen cranberries. Stir in the confectioners sugar and salt. Set aside to macerate.

3. Add all the streusel topping ingredients to the bowl of a food processor. Pulse until just combined.

4. Add ½ cup cooled pecan halves and pulse again until coarse. Put streusel topping in a small bowl and set aside.

5. Coarsely chop remaining 1¼ cups toasted pecan halves. Set aside.

6. In a small bowl, whisk together eggs, sugar, and milk. Set aside.

7. In a mixing bowl, combine flours, baking powder and salt.

Steps 3–5 can be done by hand.

8. Add coarsely chopped pecans and macerated cranberries to flour mixture. Toss to combine.

9. Whisk egg mixture again to get sugar up from the bottom.

10. Pour egg mixture over dry ingredients. Stir only a few strokes.

11. Drizzle melted butter over all.

12. Stir gently by using a rubber scraper to scrape down around the sides and up through the center with a scraping/lifting/folding motion. Stir only until mostly combined—a few streaks of flour are fine.

13. Place batter in well-greased muffin pans, filling each cup ¾ full.

14. Top with streusel topping. Press down lightly.

15. Bake in preheated 425°F oven for 12–18 minutes, until golden and springy when touched.

16. Allow muffins to cool in pan(s) for 5 minutes. Run a thin-bladed knife around each muffin. Remove from pans. Serve warm, or allow to cool and freeze.

Basic Muffins

MAKES: 12–15 muffins

PREP. TIME: 20 minutes

BAKING TIME: 18–20 minutes

1 cup whole wheat pastry flour

½ cup whole wheat bread flour

½ cup all-purpose flour

1 tsp. baking soda

¼ tsp. salt

¼ cup brown sugar, packed, *or*
   white sugar

1 cup plain lowfat yogurt,
   buttermilk, *or* thick sour milk

1 large egg, beaten

3 Tbsp. melted unsalted butter,
   or oil

1. In a large bowl, stir together the dry ingredients.

2. In another bowl, mix together yogurt and egg.

3. Pour egg mixture over dry ingredients. Stir just a few strokes.

4. Drizzle butter over all.

5. Stir gently by using a rubber scraper to scrape down around the sides and up through the center with a scraping/lifting/folding motion. Stir only until mostly combined—a few streaks of flour are fine.

6. Fill well-greased muffin cups ¾ full.

7. Bake in preheated 350°F oven for 17–20 minutes or until they spring back when lightly pressed on the top.

8. Remove to a wire rack. Cool a few minutes, then remove from the pans. Eat warm with butter and jam.

Design-Your-Own Muffins

MAKES: 12 muffins

PREP. TIME: 20 minutes

BAKING TIME: 10–15 minutes

¼ cup (half stick) unsalted butter

1 large egg, room temperature

1 cup milk (not skim), room temperature

⅓ cup sugar

¼-½ tsp. vanilla extract

1¼ cups whole wheat pastry flour

¾ cup all-purpose flour

1 Tbsp. baking powder

½ tsp. salt

These can be used as individual shortcakes. Cut them in half from the top almost through to the bottom. Lay open with the cut side up on a plate or bowl. Put a generous serving of sliced strawberries or peaches down the middle and top with whipped cream or milk.

1. Melt the butter. Set aside to cool.

2. In a bowl, thoroughly whisk the egg.

3. Whisk in the milk, sugar, and vanilla. Set aside.

4. In a large bowl, whisk together the dry ingredients.

5. Stir the egg mixture again to dissolve the sugar that settles to the bottom of the bowl. Pour egg mixture over the dry ingredients.

6. Using a flat whisk or wooden spoon, stir gently, scraping up from the bottom until halfway incorporated.

7. Add the melted butter and gently lift and stir until the batter comes together. There should be some lumps. It will be a fairly runny batter.

8. Spoon batter into well-greased and floured muffin tins.

9. Bake in preheated 375°F oven 10–15 minutes. They should spring back when touched.

10. Remove from pans.

Designer options: choose one (or more!) and do either while preparing the batter or just before baking:

- *Sprinkle with cinnamon sugar or a streusel topping.*

- *Top with 1 tsp. jam. Using a toothpick or skewer, just on the top surface, swirl it in a figure eight.*

- *Stir in ⅓ cup chopped nuts along with the dry ingredients or sprinkle them on top just before baking.*

- *Chop up dried fruit and stir it into the wet ingredients. Set it aside while you prepare the pans and remaining ingredients.*

- *Add lemon or orange zest.*

- *Omit sugar and vanilla. Toss into dry ingredients: 7 oz. chopped fresh spinach, frozen, drained and squeezed dry, or 1¼ cups crumbled bleu cheese, ½ cup oil-packed sun-dried tomatoes, drained and chopped, ½ lb. bacon, fried nearly crisp and chopped. Replace butter with extra-virgin olive oil.*

How to make your own roasted cornmeal:

Start with whole ears of corn. Field corn works fine. Remove the kernels from the ears. Clean to remove the chaff by winnowing or washing.

To winnow, set up a fan over a sheet outside. Pour the kernels from one container to another in front of the fan's breeze. The chaff will blow away. Pick up any dropped kernels from the sheet. Repeat until no more chaff blows off the corn.

To wash, wash quickly in cold water. Do not soak the kernels. Then spread on towels to dry.

Spread cleaned kernels evenly on baking sheets. Bake at 325°F, 20–30 minutes, stirring often. When they are nicely roasted, they will have a sweet roasted aroma and be lightly golden brown.

Cool. Process in a coffee grinder, food processor, or blender. Store in the refrigerator.

These are delicious and flavorful — great served with a pot of soup.

Cornmeal Muffins

MAKES: 12–15 muffins

PREP. TIME: 20 minutes

BAKING TIME: 12–18 minutes

½ cup whole wheat bread flour *

½ cup pastry flour

1 cup whole grain cornmeal, preferably roasted

2½ tsp. baking powder

1 tsp. salt

⅓ cup sugar

1 large egg

3 Tbsp. oil *or* melted butter

½ cup mayonnaise

1 cup cream-style corn

2 Tbsp. finely minced onion, *optional*

* *I sometimes use whole-grain spelt flour as part of the whole wheat flour.*

1. In a large bowl, stir together the flours, cornmeal, baking powder and salt.

2. In another bowl, whisk egg and sugar.

3. Whisk oil, mayonnaise, corn, and optional onion into the egg mixture.

4. Stir gently by using a rubber scraper to scrape down around the sides and up through the center with a scraping/lifting/folding motion. Stir only until mostly combined—a few streaks of flour are fine.

5. Place batter in well-greased muffin pans, filling each cup ¾ full.

6. Bake in preheated 425°F oven for 12–18 minutes, until golden and springy when touched.

7. Allow muffins to cool in pan(s) for 5 minutes. Run a thin-bladed knife around each muffin. Remove from pans. Serve warm, or allow to cool and freeze.

Be careful not to use Miracle Whip salad dressing in place of the mayonnaise.

I make my own cream-style corn. I put slightly thawed, home-frozen corn in the food processor, then pulse until it is mostly creamy with bits of corn in it. I do not puree it entirely.

Pumpkin Muffins

MAKES: 12 muffins

PREP. TIME: 15 minutes

BAKING TIME: 12–18 minutes

½ cup whole wheat bread
    flour

½ cup whole wheat pastry
    flour

½ cup all-purpose flour

1 tsp. ground cinnamon

½ tsp. ground ginger

¼ tsp. ground nutmeg

1 tsp. baking soda

¾ tsp. salt

2 large eggs

⅔ cup sugar

1 cup thick pumpkin puree

¼ cup oil

¼ cup water, orange juice,
    or buttermilk

cinnamon sugar, *optional*

If the consistency of your pumpkin puree is thin and runny, omit the liquid and use 1¼ cups of thin puree.

1. In large bowl, combine the flours, spices, baking soda, and salt.

2. In another bowl, lightly whisk eggs and sugar. Whisk in the pumpkin, oil and water.

3. Stir gently by using a rubber scraper to scrape down around the sides and up through the center with a scraping/lifting/folding motion. Stir only until mostly combined—a few streaks of flour are fine.

4. Place batter in well-greased muffin pans, filling each cup ¾ full. Sprinkle with cinnamon sugar if you wish.

5. Bake in preheated 425°F oven for 12–18 minutes, until golden and springy when touched.

6. Allow muffins to cool in pan for 5 minutes. Run a thin-bladed knife around each muffin. Remove from pans. Serve warm, or allow to cool and freeze.

Rhubarb Muffins

MAKES: 12 muffins

PREP. TIME: 20 minutes

BAKING TIME: 12–18 minutes

½ cup whole wheat pastry
  flour

¼ cup whole wheat bread
  flour

½ cup all-purpose flour

½ tsp. baking soda

¼ tsp. baking powder

½ tsp. ground cinnamon

scant ½ tsp. salt

1 cup chopped rhubarb,
  fresh or still frozen (not
  thawed), no larger than
  ½" dice

1 large egg

⅔ cup brown sugar, packed

scant ½ cup plain lowfat
  yogurt or thick buttermilk

⅓ cup oil

½ tsp. vanilla extract

STREUSEL:

3 Tbsp. sugar

1 tsp. ground cinnamon

1 Tbsp. unsalted butter, room
  temperature

1. In a large bowl combine the flours, baking soda, baking powder, cinnamon, and salt.

2. Stir or toss the finely diced, still frozen rhubarb into the dry ingredients.

3. In another bowl whisk the egg. Whisk in brown sugar, yogurt, oil, and vanilla.

4. Pour wet ingredients over top of dry.

5. Stir gently by using a rubber scraper to scrape down around the sides and up through the center with a scraping/lifting/folding motion. Stir only until mostly combined—a few streaks of flour are fine.

6. In a small bowl, combine streusel ingredients with the back of a spoon, pressing into crumbs.

7. Place batter in well-greased muffin pans, filling each cup ¾ full. Sprinkle with streusel. Pat streusel gently into each muffin top.

8. Bake in preheated 375°F oven for 12–18 minutes, until golden and springy when touched.

9. Allow muffins to cool in pan for 5 minutes. Run a thin-bladed knife around each muffin. Remove from pans. Serve warm, or allow to cool and freeze.

Freeze rhubarb while in season. Wash, dry, chop, and bag it. No need to heat-process rhubarb.

My niece Betsy loves all things rhubarb. These are her favorite muffins.

These are a bit involved, but well worth the effort. They can be done in stages. Make the topping and filling ahead and refrigerate. Bring to room temperature when you're ready to assemble the muffins.

Very Blueberry Muffins

MAKES: 12 muffins

PREP. TIME: 30 minutes

STANDING TIME: 20–30 minutes

BAKING TIME: 12–18 minutes

1 cup + ¼ cup + 1 tsp. sugar, *divided*

1½ tsp. finely grated lemon zest

2¼ cups blueberries, fresh *or* frozen (do not thaw), *divided*

1 cup whole wheat pastry flour

¾ cup whole wheat bread flour

¾ cup all-purpose flour

2½ tsp. baking powder

¾ tsp. salt

2 large eggs, room temperature

¼ cup (half stick) unsalted butter, melted, cooled slightly

¼ cup oil

1 cup plain lowfat yogurt, room temperature

½ tsp. vanilla extract

Steps 1 and 2 can be done ahead and refrigerated.

1. In a small bowl, stir together the ¼ cup sugar and lemon zest. Cover and set aside.

2. In a small heavy kettle, combine 1¼ cups of the blueberries with 1 tsp. sugar. Mash slightly with the back of a spoon to release the juices. Stir and simmer for 4–7 minutes until thickened and reduced to a scant ⅓ cup. Set aside to cool.

3. In a large bowl whisk the flours, baking powder, and salt. Stir in the remaining 1 cup blueberries. Set aside.

4. In another bowl whisk the eggs and remaining 1 cup sugar until thick and lemon-colored. Slowly whisk in the butter and oil.

5. Whisk in room-temperature yogurt and vanilla until combined.

6. Pour wet ingredients over dry.

7. Stir gently by using a rubber scraper to scrape down around the sides and up through the center with a scraping/lifting/folding motion. Stir only until mostly combined—a few streaks of flour are fine.

8. Place batter in well-greased muffin pans, filling each cup ¾ full.

9. Dollop the reduced, cooled blueberry mixture on top of each muffin. Use a skewer to gently poke the filling, then swirl a figure 8. The filling should be slightly mixed into the muffins, but still on top.

10. If using frozen blueberries, let the filled muffins set 15 minutes to thaw slightly.

11. Sprinkle tops with lemon sugar from Step 1.

12. Bake in preheated 400°F oven for 12–18 minutes, until golden and springy when touched.

13. Allow muffins to cool in pan for 5 minutes. Run a thin-bladed knife around each muffin. Remove from pans. Serve warm, or allow to cool and freeze.

Apple Streusel Muffins

MAKES: 10–12 muffins

PREP. TIME: 20 minutes

BAKING TIME: 10–15 minutes

STREUSEL:

3 Tbsp. sugar

1 Tbsp. whole grain spelt flour *or* whole wheat pastry flour

1 tsp. ground cinnamon

1 Tbsp. unsalted butter, softened

½ cup whole wheat pastry flour

⅓ cup whole wheat bread flour

¼ cup all-purpose flour

½ tsp. ground cinnamon

1½ tsp. baking powder

½ tsp. baking soda

¼ tsp. salt

¾–1 cup finely chopped tart apples, peeling optional *

1 large egg, room temperature

½ cup sugar

⅓ cup thick applesauce, room temperature

½ tsp. vanilla extract

¼ cup (half stick) unsalted butter, melted, cooled

* If all you have on hand are sweet non-baking apples, stir 1 tsp. lemon juice into the chopped apples and allow to macerate while you mix up the muffins.

1. In a small bowl combine the streusel ingredients, pressing and scraping with the flat side of a spoon or small spatula until crumb-like. Set aside.

2. In a large bowl mix the dry ingredients. Stir in the chopped apples. Set aside.

3. In another bowl lightly beat the egg. Add the sugar and beat 30 seconds. Add the applesauce and vanilla. Mix thoroughly.

4. Pour the egg mixture over the dry ingredients.

5. Using a rubber spatula, stir a few strokes to halfway combine, scraping down the sides, across the bottom and up through the dry ingredients. Drizzle on the butter and stir until just combined—a few streaks of flour are fine.

6. Place batter in well-greased muffin pans, filling each cup ¾ full.

7. Divide streusel topping evenly over each muffin. Pat lightly.

8. Bake in preheated 400°F oven for 10–15 minutes, until golden and springy when touched.

9. Allow muffins to cool in pan for 5 minutes. Run a thin-bladed knife around each muffin. Remove from pans. Serve warm, or allow to cool and freeze.

This is a good recipe to use up some leftover applesauce that is just starting to sour a bit. It enhances the flavor of the muffins. It gives added flavor like buttermilk or sour milk does.

Lemon Poppyseed Muffins

These muffins are a bit more like cake than traditional muffins — very tender and lightly sweetened.

MAKES: 12 muffins

PREP. TIME: 30 minutes

BAKING/COOKING TIME: 15–21 minutes

½ cup whole wheat bread flour

½ cup whole wheat pastry flour

½ cup all-purpose flour

1½ tsp. baking powder

½ tsp. baking soda

¼ tsp. salt

1½ Tbsp. poppy seeds

2–3 tsp. finely grated lemon zest

¼ cup (half stick) unsalted butter, room temperature

½ cup + 2 Tbsp. sugar, *divided*

1 large egg

¾ cup plain lowfat yogurt *or* thick buttermilk

3 Tbsp. fresh lemon juice

1. In a large bowl stir together flours, baking powder, baking soda, salt, poppy seeds, and lemon zest.
2. In another bowl, cream the butter until light and fluffy.
3. Add ½ cup sugar and beat until light and fluffy. Add the egg. Beat well.
4. Add ⅓ of the dry ingredients and half of the yogurt. Combine. Repeat.
5. Add remaining dry ingredients. Mix until flour is incorporated.
6. Fill well-greased muffin pans ¾ full.
7. Bake in preheated 350°F oven for 12–18 minutes or until golden and springy when touched.
8. Cool 5 minutes in the muffin tin. Run a thin-bladed knife around each muffin. Remove from pans to wire racks.
9. While the muffins are baking and then cooling, combine the lemon juice and the remaining 2 Tbsp. sugar in a small pan.
10. Stir and cook until slightly syrupy.
11. Remove glaze from pan to a small bowl to cool a bit.
12. Brush glaze evenly on the tops of the slightly warm muffins.

Orange Muffins

MAKES: 12 muffins

PREP. TIME: 20 minutes

BAKING TIME: 12–18 minutes

STREUSEL:

2 Tbsp. sugar

2 Tbsp. brown sugar

1–2 tsp. orange zest

2 tsp. unsalted butter, room temperature, *optional*

¾ cup whole wheat pastry flour

½ cup whole wheat bread flour

¾ cup all-purpose flour

2 tsp. baking powder

½ tsp. baking soda

¾ tsp. salt

1 Tbsp. orange zest

½ cup toasted, chopped walnuts

1 large egg, room temperature

½ cup sugar

⅔ cup orange juice, room temperature

½ cup (1 stick) unsalted butter, melted, cooled

You may add up to ½ cup dried fruit (cranberries, apricots, golden raisins, etc.) as desired.

1. In a small bowl combine the sugars and the orange zest to make the streusel. Stir in optional butter using the back of a spoon until evenly combined. Set aside.

2. In a large bowl, stir together flours, baking powder, baking soda, and salt. Stir in orange zest and walnuts.

3. In another bowl, lightly whisk the egg. Whisk in sugar, orange juice, and melted, cooled butter.

4. Pour over the dry ingredients.

5. Stir gently by using a rubber scraper to scrape down around the sides and up through the center with a scraping/lifting/folding motion. Stir only until mostly combined—a few streaks of flour are fine.

6. Place batter in well-greased muffin pans, filling each cup ¾ full.

7. Divide streusel topping evenly over each muffin. Pat streusel gently into muffin top.

8. Bake in preheated 375°F oven for 12–18 minutes, until golden and springy when touched.

9. Allow muffins to cool in pan for 5 minutes. Run a thin-bladed knife around each muffin. Remove from pans. Serve warm, or allow to cool and freeze.

Cinnamon Topped Oatmeal Muffins

MAKES: 12 muffins

PREP. TIME: 20 minutes

STANDING TIME: 25–30 minutes

BAKING TIME: 10–15 minutes

½ cup whole wheat bread flour

½ cup whole wheat pastry flour

1¼ cups quick *or* rolled oats

3 tsp. baking powder

½ tsp. salt

½ cup chopped raisins, dried cranberries, *or* dried fruit of your choice

1 tsp. ground cinnamon, *optional*

1 large egg

1 cup milk

¼ cup sugar

3 Tbsp. oil *or* melted butter

TOPPING:

2 Tbsp. sugar

1 Tbsp. whole wheat pastry flour

½–1 tsp. ground cinnamon

1 tsp. unsalted butter, room temperature

1. In bowl combine flours, oats, baking powder, salt, chopped fruit, and optional cinnamon.

2. In another bowl, thoroughly whisk the egg. Whisk in the milk and sugar.

3. Pour milk mixture over the oat mixture. Stir to combine. Let sit for 15 minutes for quick oats, 20 minutes for rolled oats.

4. Put topping ingredients in a small bowl. Mash with the back of a spoon until completely combined and crumbly. Set aside.

5. Add the oil to the oat mixture and stir just until combined.

6. Fill greased muffin cups ¾ full. Let sit 10 minutes longer.

7. Sprinkle topping over the muffin tops. Pat topping gently into each muffin.

8. Bake in preheated 425°F oven for 10–15 minutes or until springy and a bit golden.

9. Allow muffins to cool in pan for 5 minutes. Run a thin-bladed knife around each muffin. Remove from pans. Serve warm, or allow to cool and freeze.

1. **Mix pancakes in a bowl that has ample stirring room with gently sloped sides.** To incorporate the dry and wet ingredients, **use a large flat whisk** to scrape down the sides and up the middle, turning the bowl as you work. Make sure to pick up all the dry ingredients in the bottom of the bowl. Finish the mixing with just one or two stirs throughout the batter. The less mixing, the more tender the pancakes.

2. **To properly measure flour** see page 124.

3. **Have your ingredients at room temperature** to prevent unnecessary cooling of your griddle or waffle maker. If I'm in a hurry, I microwave the milk enough to take the chill off.

4. Some like pancakes thick; some like them thin. **Try adding less buttermilk for thicker pancakes, and more for thinner.** It also depends on the thickness of your buttermilk. Sometimes my buttermilk is runny, so I add as much as ¼ cup less per batch if I want a thicker pancake.

5. **You can add fruit to any pancake batter.** I prefer to stir firm fruits (finely diced apples and blueberries, for example) into the dry ingredients before adding the wet ingredients. Or sprinkle them on top of the pancakes immediately after pouring the batter onto the griddle.

6. **Serve pancakes and waffles** with plain or Greek yogurt, a variety of fresh or frozen thawed fruits, chopped nuts, and a splash of syrup (if you think it necessary along with all the other toppings). This makes a most satisfying breakfast that is really quite fit for royalty.

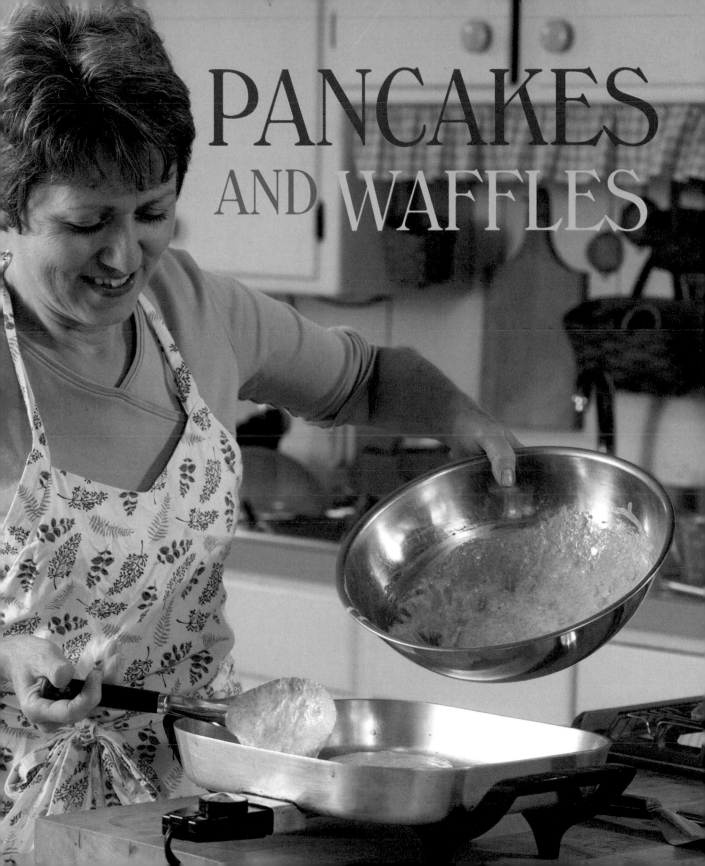

PANCAKES
AND WAFFLES

These are the pancakes that I make most of the time. The available fruits for toppings make them different every time.

My Favorite Pancakes

MAKES: 6–7 medium pancakes

PREP. TIME: 15 minutes

COOKING TIME: 5–7 minutes per pancake

1½ cups whole wheat pastry flour *or* whole grain spelt flour, *or* combination *

½ cup pastry flour

1 tsp. baking powder

½ tsp. baking soda

½ tsp. salt

2 Tbsp. ground flax seed, *optional*

2 cups thick buttermilk or plain yogurt, room temperature or slightly warmed

2 eggs, room temperature, lightly beaten

2 Tbsp. oil or melted butter

* *You can increase the whole grains to all whole wheat. The pancakes will get a bit heavier, but they're delicious.*

1. In a large bowl, stir together flours, baking powder, baking soda, salt, and optional flax seed.

2. Add buttermilk and egg. Stir a few strokes.

3. Add oil and mix gently until just barely combined. Minimum stirring makes tender pancakes! The batter will be fairly thick (although a thinner buttermilk will make a thinner batter).

4. Heat lightly oiled skillet on medium-high heat until a few drops of water skitter across the skillet before evaporating.

5. Spoon batter onto hot greased skillet. When pancakes are getting a bit dry around the edges and a bubble or two appears in the middle, flip and cook a minute or two longer, until done in the middle.

Mix the dry ingredients together ahead of time. Store in the freezer. It's your own pancake mix without any preservatives!

You can halve or double this recipe.

For sweet milk pancakes, omit the baking soda. Use 1½ cups whole milk in place of the buttermilk.

Increase or decrease the liquid for thicker or thinner pancakes.

Oatmeal Pancakes

M y family calls these "baked oatmeal, pancake-style."

MAKES: 3–4 servings

PREP. TIME: 15 minutes

STANDING TIME: 8 hours or overnight

COOKING TIME: 5–7 minutes per pancake

2 cups rolled oats

½ cup plain lowfat yogurt or buttermilk

1½ cups water

2 large eggs, beaten

¼ cup oil *or* melted butter

½ cup whole wheat pastry flour *or* whole grain spelt flour

2 Tbsp. sugar

2 tsp. baking powder

1 tsp. baking soda

¼ tsp. ground cinnamon, more or less to taste

½ tsp. salt

1. Mix together oats, yogurt and water. Cover. Allow to sit at room temperature for 8 hours or overnight.

2. Stir in the beaten eggs and oil.

3. Separately, stir together the dry ingredients.

4. Stir dry ingredients into oat mixture with just a few strokes. A few streaks of flour may remain. Minimum stirring makes tender pancakes!

5. Heat lightly oiled skillet on medium-high heat until a few drops of water skitter across the skillet before evaporating.

6. Spoon batter onto hot greased skillet. When pancakes are getting a bit dry around the edges and a bubble or two appears in the middle, flip and cook a minute or two longer, until done in the middle.

Buckwheat Pancakes

MAKES: 3–4 servings

PREP. TIME: 15 minutes

COOKING TIME: 5–7 minutes per pancake

1 cup buckwheat flour

1 cup whole grain spelt flour *or* whole wheat pastry flour

2–3 Tbsp. brown *or* white sugar

½ tsp. baking soda

2 tsp. baking powder

¾ tsp. salt

1¼ cups buttermilk *or* sour milk

1 large egg, beaten

2 Tbsp. melted unsalted butter *or* oil

1. In a large bowl, mix both flours, sugar, baking soda, baking powder, and salt.

2. In another bowl whisk together the buttermilk and egg.

3. Pour the milk mixture over the dry ingredients and stir slightly.

4. Add the oil and stir until just combined. A few streaks of flour may remain. Minimum stirring makes tender pancakes!

5. Heat lightly oiled skillet on medium-high heat until a few drops of water skitter across the skillet before evaporating.

6. Spoon batter onto hot greased skillet. When pancakes are getting a bit dry around the edges and a bubble or two appears in the middle, flip and cook a minute or two longer, until done in the middle.

Variation:

- For fluffier waffles, separate the eggs. Beat the yolks and add them with the milk. Beat the whites until stiff and fold them in last.

Whole Wheat Waffles

MAKES: about 3 8" square waffles

PREP. TIME: 20 minutes

COOKING TIME: about 2 minutes a waffle

1½ cups whole wheat pastry flour, may use part whole grain spelt flour

½ cup pastry flour

2 tsp. baking powder

1 tsp. baking soda

½ tsp. salt

2 cups buttermilk, thick sour milk *or* plain lowfat yogurt

2 large eggs, beaten

6 Tbsp. melted butter, bacon grease, lard, or neutral oil. (My preference is half butter/half bacon grease.)

1. Preheat waffle iron.

2. In a large bowl, stir together the dry ingredients.

3. Add buttermilk and beaten eggs and stir slightly.

4. Add butter and stir together until just combined. A few streaks of flour may remain. Minimum stirring makes tender waffles!

5. Lightly grease the hot waffle maker with a pastry brush and oil or non-stick baking spray before baking the first waffle or two.

6. Use a ladle or large spoon to quickly add the amount of batter required for your waffle iron to the center of the grids. Don't overfill. Use the back of the ladle to slightly spread the batter around. It will level and spread itself as it bakes.

7. Close the iron as quickly as possible to avoid cooling. When the hissing/steaming slows, (approximately 2 minutes) carefully lift the lid. Use a sharp fork to lift the waffle at the corner. Grab the waffle with a salad tongs (or your fingers, ouch!) and remove the waffle to a wire rack.

8. Close the waffle iron immediately and allow it to come back to full heat before adding more batter.

9. Repeat until batter is finished.

If your waffle iron is new, you will want to grease it well before **each** *waffle the first several times you use it. The heat and the grease will establish the seasoning. After you've achieved a good seasoning, you shouldn't have to grease it much at all.*

Never *scrub your waffle iron grids in hot sudsy water. Doing so removes the seasoning and causes much sticking of waffles and frustration the next time you make waffles. After a waffle-making session, I simply wipe off any drips and crumbs on the outside and store the waffle iron covered with a clean cloth to prevent dust build-up.*

Pumpkin Spice Waffles

MAKES: 12 4" waffles

PREP. TIME: 20 minutes

COOKING TIME: about 2 minutes per waffle

1¼ cups whole wheat pastry flour

½ cup pastry flour

2 tsp. baking powder

½ tsp. salt

1 tsp. baking soda

1 tsp. ground cinnamon

½ tsp. ground ginger

⅛ tsp. ground nutmeg

2 large eggs, room temperature

1 cup pumpkin puree

1¼ cups buttermilk, room temperature *

¼ cup brown sugar *or* white sugar

6 Tbsp. oil

* If you don't have buttermilk, use plain milk and omit the baking soda.

> *As a variation, sprinkle finely chopped nuts on the unbaked waffle before closing the lid.*

1. Preheat waffle iron.
2. In a large bowl, stir together the dry ingredients.
3. In another bowl, whisk the eggs. Whisk in the pumpkin, buttermilk, sugar and oil.
4. Pour egg mixture over dry ingredients. Whisk just until combined — streaks of flour are fine.
5. Lightly grease the hot waffle maker with a pastry brush and oil or non-stick baking spray before baking the first waffle or two.
6. Use a ladle or large spoon to quickly add the amount of batter required for your waffle iron to the center of the grids. Don't overfill. Use the back of the ladle to slightly spread the batter around. It will level and spread itself as it bakes.
7. Close the iron as quickly as possible to avoid cooling. When the hissing/steaming slows (approximately 2 minutes), carefully lift the lid. Use a sharp fork to lift the waffle at the corner. Grab the waffle with a salad tongs (or your fingers, ouch!) and remove the waffle to a wire rack.
8. Close the waffle iron immediately and allow it to come back to full heat before adding more batter.
9. Repeat until batter is finished.

Simple Homemade Pancake Syrup

Think of all the plastic syrup jugs you won't be adding to the landfills!

MAKES: 3 cups

PREP. TIME: 5 minutes

COOKING TIME: 10 minutes

COOLING TIME: 30 minutes

2 cups water *

2 cups white sugar

½ cup brown sugar, packed

⅓ tsp. maple flavoring

⅔ tsp. vanilla extract

* *Over the years, I've increased the original 1 cup water to 2¼ cups of water without increasing the amount of sugar. I did it so gradually that nobody complained or appeared to notice the difference. To break your gang in, start with 1 cup water as it does make a thicker syrup. Very gradually, over time, add water to a point that is acceptable to you.*

1. Place the water and sugars in a 2-quart heavy bottom pan. Stir.
2. Cover. Bring to a boil over medium heat, stirring once or twice.
3. Turn to low and simmer, covered, for 5 minutes. Simmering while covered prevents the sugars from crystallizing during storage.
4. Take covered pan off heat and allow to cool for at least 30 minutes, still covered.
5. Add maple and vanilla extracts.
6. Store in a jar in the refrigerator. Keeps for months.

As you use up the syrup, store it in smaller jars to help keep it fresh. Since there are no preservatives, never mix an older batch with a new batch for long-term storage.

I keep a mixture of one part maple flavoring and 2 parts vanilla extract stored in a small flavoring bottle. Use 1 tsp. of this mixture for the full batch. Write the recipe amounts on tape and stick it onto the side of the bottle. No searching for the recipe.

If a batch threatens to go bad, skim off any mold. Boil and cool the syrup. Freeze it to use in your next batch of granola. Decrease the sugar in the granola.

1. **A Pizza and Pastry Dual Rolling Pin is the best rolling pin I've found for working with an oil crust.** It doesn't cause the wax paper to buckle as much.

2. **Choose an oil or fat that enhances whatever filling you're using.** You can use part or all extra-virgin olive oil for quiches and main dish crusts.

3. **Glass or pottery pie plates are easiest to work with** because their weight keeps them from sliding around on the countertop when you're arranging the rolled crust. These recipes are for regular (not deep-dish) 9″ pie pans. Vintage pie pans are usually smaller or more shallow than modern pans.

4. **When making oil pie crusts, crimp the edges right away because this dough sets up quickly and soon is no longer pliable.** If you're making a double-crust pie and have the ingredients ready to put into the bottom crust, you'll have enough time to put the top crust on.

5. **To make double-crust pies with a cooked filling,** prepare your filling and let it cool as you assemble your crusts. Your filling ingredients must be barely warm so that you can work with the top crust.

   Fill the pie; then form the top crust and place it over all. Crimp the top and bottom crust edges together immediately. Use a skewer or the tip of a paring knife to poke or slash 5 or 6 vent holes to allow the steam to escape while baking. You don't want your pie to explode in the oven.

6. **Most pie recipes call for a very hot oven—425–450° F—for the first 8–10 minutes,** then back down to 350° for the remainder of the time. The high temperature at the beginning bakes the crust quickly. Lowering the temperature finishes the baking more evenly.

   For a homemade appearance, I like when the fruit filling has bubbled up into the crimped edge at just a few spots. These whole wheat crusts will look toasty brown even before baking, so don't go by browning as an indicator of doneness.

7. **Fruit pies, with the exception of apple pies, get better with age.** A day or two does a lot for the flavor.

8. **Do not store fruit pies in airtight containers!** The moisture from the filling makes the crumbs and crust soggy. Cover them with a tea towel and store them in a pantry, or, as my sister-in-law does, on top of the plates and dishes in the cupboard. My handy husband made me stacking wooden pie-plate holders. I have no excuse for not making lots of pies at once. We love pie!

Confession: We eat pie for breakfast.

PIES

Crumb Topping

MAKES: about 4 cups. This is enough crumbs for about 8 pies. Use ⅓–½ cup per pie.

PREP. TIME: 15 minutes

2 cups whole wheat pastry flour *or part whole grain spelt flour or oat flour* *

½ cup sugar (either all granulated, all brown, or a combination of the two)

2 sticks butter, softened

Pinch of salt if using unsalted butter

1. In a bowl, combine flours and sugars.
2. Add softened butter. Use your fingers to rub into fine crumbs.
3. Place crumbs in a jar or other airtight container and store in the freezer for future use.

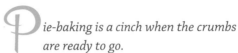

Add ground nuts for added protein and flavor.

P ie-baking is a cinch when the crumbs are ready to go.

Basic Oil Pie Crust

MAKES: 9" crust

¾ cup whole wheat pastry flour

¼ cup + 2 Tbsp. pastry flour

¼–½ tsp. table salt

4 Tbsp. neutral oil. (I prefer peanut oil for optimal flavor.)

2 Tbsp. cold water

This recipe came from my mother-in-law. She made the most tender pie crusts imaginable. I was never crazy about the flavor of this crust until I experimented using oils and fats other than vegetable oil. This is when this crust really got flavorful!

1. Mix together flours and salt in a large bowl.
2. Using a table fork, stir in the oil until flour is completely mixed in.
3. Add water. Toss with the fork *just* until it comes together into a cohesive ball, stopping once to scrape the bowl. It will look slimy at first before it gathers together. Do not over stir.
4. Cut 2 12" squares of waxed paper. (The width of a roll is 12".)
5. Form the ball of dough into a round flat disc. Place disc in the center of one piece of waxed paper. Press evenly with your hands to get it as big as you can and still have it even with no cracks.
6. Center and press the second piece of waxed paper on top of dough disc, having the edges even.
7. Using a Pastry and Pizza dual rolling pin (see page xxiv) roll the dough into an even circle. Spin it around to your advantage, even pick it up and hold the sandwiched dough to the light to check for thick and thin spots. Place it back on the counter and use the rolling pin to pull dough from the thick spots to fill in the thin spots.
8. When the circle of dough is ¼" from the edges of the waxed paper, it is the right size for an average 9" glass pie plate.
9. Carefully peel off the top layer of waxed paper.
10. Pick up the bottom waxed paper with the crust on it and turn it upside down over the pie plate, centering it. You can move the crust gently as long as one waxed paper is still on it.
11. Pinch the 2 corners of the waxed paper farthest from you. Slowly peel the paper off by pulling out and towards yourself.
12. Do not press the crust into the pan or it will stick. Gently lift the edges of the crust until it is fully lowered and settled in the pie pan. Crimp edges.

I find that the crust is flaky enough using 4 Tbsp. oil, but if you want an extra tender pie crust, add another tablespoon.

Basic Oil Pie Crust Variations

Room temperature (very soft) lard can be used in place of the oil. It makes a super-tender, delicious crust. It is challenging to work with, so get familiar with making oil crusts before you use lard. Other ingredients must be warm to room temperature also.

For a pie crust with more body, use up to half whole wheat bread flour. The rest of the flour must be either whole wheat pastry flour or pastry flour. The added gluten gives the crust more structure. It can become tough if it's overworked.

Whole grain spelt flour can be used as part of the flour in pie crusts. Because of the added protein content, use ½ cup whole grain spelt flour, ¼ cup plus 2 Tbsp. whole wheat pastry flour and ¼ cup pastry flour.

Some people eat pie for the crust. If you like a thicker crust use:

    1 cup whole wheat pastry flour
    ½ cup pastry flour
    ½ tsp. salt
    ⅓ cup oil
    2½–3 Tbsp. cold water

I find that this recipe works well for prebaked crusts. Using a sharp-tined fork or a toothpick, poke holes about 1½" apart all over the prepared crust. Bake in a preheated 425°F oven until golden and baked all over, 10–12 minutes. If the crust does bubble up during baking, poke the bubble with a pin to release the air before it sets up.

Pie crusts, baked or unbaked, freeze well. Wrap each plate containing a pie crust individually. Freeze for up to 1 month. They are very fragile; use care when moving things around in the freezer.

Shoofly Pie

MAKES: 9" pie

¾ cup whole wheat pastry
  flour

¼ cup pastry flour

½ cup brown sugar, packed

1 Tbsp. salted butter,
  softened

1 cup hot water

1 tsp. baking soda

1 cup King Syrup

1 large egg, beaten

9" unbaked pie crust

1. In large bowl, mix both flours and
brown sugar.

2. Cut in the butter with fingers or
flat whisk until you get the texture
of cornmeal. Set aside ⅔ cup for
topping.

3. Separately, add baking soda to hot water in a large
mixing bowl. It will foam up. Stir to dissolve.

4. Add rest of ingredients to baking soda mixture.
Whisk well to combine.

5. Pour wet ingredients into the flour mixture. Whisk
to combine; the batter will be runny.

6. Be sure the pie shell does not have cracks in the
edges—it is going to be very full. Pour batter into
pie shell.

7. Sprinkle reserved ⅔ cup crumbs on top.

8. Bake at 375°F for 35–40 minutes or until set up in
the middle. It should spring back like a cake when
touched. If it seems to be getting browned before it
is set up, cut the heat back to 350°F.

*For more
flavor, use
up to ¼ cup
green label
Brer Rabbit
Molasses.
Descrease the
King Syrup by
¼ cup.*

My Mother-in-Law's Apple Pie Filling

MAKES: a 9" pie

PREP. TIME: 25 minutes

COOKING/BAKING TIME: 45–50 minutes

1 piled high quart peeled, cored and thinly sliced baking apples, 4–6 apples, shaken and tapped down to prevent air pockets *

1 Tbsp. fresh lemon juice, *optional*; use it if your apples aren't tart baking apples.

4 Tbsp. water (5 if no lemon juice is used)

¾–1 cup sugar (go by the sweetness of the apples)

scant ¼ tsp. salt

½–¾ tsp. ground cinnamon, *optional*

2 Tbsp. Clear Jel (not instant) or cornstarch

1 Tbsp. butter

½–¾ cup crumb topping (see page 105)

* *I prefer a mix of apples for a more flavorful pie. Any combination of tart baking apples is good. If your apples are sweet eating apples or a bit "over the hill," use the fresh lemon juice.*

1. Place apples in a heavy bottom skillet with plenty of room.

2. Add water and optional lemon juice.

3. Stir together sugar, cinnamon, salt and thickener. Add mixture to apples.

4. Cook over medium heat. Use a large flat-edge spoon to lift and mix as the apples cook, being careful not to break up the apple slices.

5. When the filling is boiling but the apples still hold their shape, turn off the heat. Stir in the butter. Pour into prepared crust.

6. Sprinkle with desired amount of crumbs.

7. Bake immediately in preheated 450°F oven for 10 minutes. Reduce heat to 350°F and bake 15–20 minutes longer or until a toothpick easily goes into an apple near the center. If the apple filling is puffing up and boiling out, it is probably a bit overbaked. You want soft, but intact, pieces of apple, not applesauce pie.

You can cook enough filling for 2 pies as long as your skillet has enough extra room to stir.

This was what we called apple dumplings when I was growing up. My mom would make four or five of these pies. We would put a slice in a bowl and pour milk over it and that was Saturday evening supper. I have fond memories of being able to eat as much as we wanted. With seven of us around the table, those pies didn't last long.

My Mother's Apple Pie Filling

MAKES: a 9" pie

PREP. TIME: 20 minutes

BAKING TIME: 30–40 minutes

COOLING TIME: 10 minutes or more

1 quart (4 cups) peeled, cored, and thinly sliced tart baking apples, 4–6 apples

1 cup sugar

⅓ cup all-purpose flour

½ cup water

½–1 tsp. ground cinnamon

dash salt

unbaked 9" pie shell and top crust (see page 106)

1. In a large bowl, stir together apples, sugar, flour, water, cinnamon, and salt.

2. Pour into prepared pie shell.

3. Add top crust. Crimp edges to seal crusts together. Make a few slashes across the top for vent holes.

4. Bake in preheated 450°F oven for 12 minutes. Reduce heat to 350°F. Bake 25–35 minutes longer until apples in the center are soft when poked with a toothpick. The juices must be bubbling for the flour to thicken properly.

5. Allow to cool at least 20 minutes before serving.

This is a recipe that I came up with at Thanksgiving when I wanted to serve a variety of pies. I had an orange to use up and the lemon sugar was left over from another baking project. My family loved the combination of orange in the filling and the hint of lemon on the top. It was just as good, if not better, the next day.

Cranberry Apple Crumb Pie

MAKES: a 9" pie

PREP. TIME: 30 minutes

BAKING TIME: 22–30 minutes

¼–½ tsp. lemon zest

3 generous cups peeled, thinly sliced, tart baking apples

1 cup + 3 Tbsp. sugar, *divided*

2 Tbsp. Clear Jel (not instant) *or* cornstarch

2 Tbsp. orange juice *or* water

½ tsp. orange zest

¼ tsp. salt

¼–½ tsp. ground cinnamon, *optional*

1¼ cup cranberries, fresh *or* frozen

¾ cup topping crumbs (see page 105)

unbaked 9" pie shell (see page 106)

1. In a small bowl, with the back of a spoon, press the lemon zest into 3 Tbsp. sugar until the consistency of wet sand. Set aside.
2. Place apples in heavy bottom skillet or saucepan.
3. Add remaining 1 cup sugar, cornstarch, orange juice, orange zest, salt, and optional cinnamon.
4. Stir and cook over medium heat until bubbly and clear.
5. Off the heat, gently fold in the cranberries.
6. Pour into prepared pie shell. Top with crumbs.
7. Sprinkle lemon sugar from Step 1 on top.
8. Bake in preheated 450°F oven for 10–12 minutes. Reduce heat to 350°F and bake for 12–18 minutes, until bubbly and golden.

When measuring sliced apples, make sure there aren't large air pockets as you slice the apples into your quart measure.

We have found that the flavor of cherry pies gets better with age. I like to bake them 1–2 days before serving them. Warm them slightly if desired.

When in season, we pick sour cherries to preserve. Here's what we do: Wash, thoroughly drain, and chill them. Remove the pits, stir in ½ cup sugar per quart of cherries, and then pack them into quart freezer containers. They keep their redness better this way. I add any remaining sugar when I cook the filling.

Reserve the cherry juices that collect in the bottom of the pan when you are pitting the cherries. Strain through a jelly bag to make delicious cherry jelly.

This is a guide to get you started. The thickness of the pie filling depends on how juicy your cherries are.

Cherry Pie

MAKES: a 9" pie

PREP. TIME: 20 minutes

COOKING/BAKING TIME: 30–35
   minutes

1 quart (a bit scant) frozen
   sour cherries, thawed

1 cup sugar (less if the
   cherries are already
   sweetened)

3½ Tbsp. Clear Jel (not
   instant) or cornstarch

scant ¼ tsp. salt

1 Tbsp. unsalted butter

¼-½ tsp. almond extract
   (not flavoring)

¾ cup pie topping crumbs
   (see page 105)

unbaked 9" pie shell
   (see page 106)

1. Place cherries, sugar, thickener, and salt in a heavy saucepan.
2. Stir together and cook stirring constantly over medium heat until boiling and thickened, 5–10 minutes.
3. Remove from the heat and stir in the butter and almond extract.
4. Pour into prepared 9" pie shell. Top with crumbs.
5. Bake in preheated 450°F oven for 10 minutes. Reduce the heat to 350°F and bake 10–15 minutes until bubbly. Cool on wire rack.

Cook pie fillings thickened with cornstarch or Clear Jel over medium heat. I'm not sure why, but cornstarch products thicken better when brought to a boil gradually.

Blueberry Pie

MAKES: a 9" pie

PREP. TIME: 20 minutes

COOKING/BAKING TIME: 30–35 minutes

3½ cups blueberries, fresh or frozen

¾–1 cup sugar

3 Tbsp. Clear Jel (not instant) *or* cornstarch

1 Tbsp. fresh lemon juice

¼ tsp. salt

2 Tbsp. water

unbaked 9" pie shell (see page 106)

¾ cup pie topping crumbs (see page 105)

1 Tbsp. butter

1. Place the blueberries, sugar, and thickener in a heavy bottom saucepan. Stir.
2. Add lemon juice, salt, and water.
3. Bring to a full boil over medium heat, stirring constantly. Remove from the heat. Stir in the butter.
4. Pour into prepared 9" pie shell. Top with crumbs.
5. Bake in preheated 450°F oven for 10 minutes. Reduce heat to 350°F and bake 10–15 minutes longer or until bubbly and golden around the edges.

If you washed your blueberries before freezing them, there is probably extra water already frozen with them. Omit the 2 Tbsp. of water.

Pumpkin Pie

MAKES: a 9" pie

PREP. TIME: 15 minutes

BAKING TIME: 25–37 minutes

COOLING TIME: at least 1 hour

1¾ cup thick pumpkin puree

1¼ cups evaporated milk

1 extra-large egg, beaten

⅔ cup sugar

1 tsp. ground cinnamon

½ tsp. ground ginger

scant ¼ tsp. ground nutmeg

½ tsp. salt

unbaked 9" pie shell (see page 106)

1. Combine the pumpkin, milk and egg. Whisk thoroughly.

2. Add sugar, cinnamon, ginger, nutmeg and salt. Whisk until thoroughly combined.

3. Pour filling in pie shell.

4. Bake in preheated 450°F oven for 10–12 minutes. Lower heat to 325°F and bake 15–25 minutes longer or until the center is just set. When you gently shake the pie it should not be liquid-y in the middle. It will continue to set up as it cools.

5. Cool completely, at least 1 hour, before serving.

To make 1¼ cups evaporated milk, enough for this pie, place 2½ cups milk in a heavy 1-quart saucepan. Bring milk to a boil uncovered. Watch closely because it can boil over suddenly. Simmer uncovered until reduced to the desired amount, 1¼ cups in this case.

Every so often, I pull the skin to one side with a fork so that the milk can evaporate more quickly. When it's done, pour only the milk into a heatproof measuring cup. Discard the skin and don't scrape the graininess from the bottom of the pan.

I'm a great fan of using "scratch" eggs from backyard chickens, but there are some recipes that taste better using the pale yellow eggs, "factory eggs" we call them, that you get at the grocery store. This is one recipe where I recommend using commercially grown eggs.

Lemon Sponge Pie

MAKES: a 9" pie

PREP. TIME: 25 minutes

BAKING TIME: 45–55 minutes

1 cup sugar

2 Tbsp. unsalted butter, room temperature

3 large eggs, room temperature

3 Tbsp. all-purpose flour

½ tsp. salt

⅓ cup fresh lemon juice (about 2 lemons)

zest of 2 lemons *

1¼ cups milk, warmed

unbaked 9" pie shell (see page 106)

* *When making zest, remove just the outer yellow part of the lemon. The white part adds an unpleasant bitterness.*

1. In a mixing bowl, cream butter and sugar.

2. Separate eggs, adding yolks to butter mixture and reserving whites in a separate large mixing bowl.

3. Beat butter mixture and egg yolks well.

4. Stir in the flour, salt, lemon juice and zest.

5. Stir in the warmed milk.

6. Beat the egg whites until they hold stiff peaks.

7. Drizzle the butter/yolk mixture over the beaten egg whites. Gently fold in until mixed.

8. Pour mixture into pie shell.

9. Bake 5 minutes in preheated 450°F oven, then reduce heat to 300°F and bake 40–50 minutes longer or until set in the middle. A wooden toothpick inserted in the middle should come out clean.

10. Cool on a wire rack.

Egg whites will beat into loftier peaks if you are careful not to get any of the yolk mixed in, and if you beat them at room temperature in a warmed, perfectly clean and dry glass, copper, or stainless steel bowl. Plastic or wood bowls trap oils, preventing high peaks from forming in egg whites.

1. **Most quick bread flavors improve overnight.** Be patient and try it.

2. **Proper mixing of quick breads is very important.** Like muffins, the batter should be stirred minimally. Lumps and some streaks of flour are better than mixing the whole way.

   To mix, first combine your dry ingredients in a large bowl. Add nuts, fruit, etc. into the dry ingredients. Toss with a fork to combine. Then add the wet mixture. Using a flexible rubber spatula, scrape down the sides and across the bottom, then lift up through the middle. Repeat several times around the bowl until the ingredients are barely incorporated. Spoon or pour into your prepared pans.

3. **Any quick bread recipe can be divided into small loaf pans.** Grease and flour your pans or line with parchment paper. Loaf pan sizes vary so much it's hard to be specific. The measurement needs to be from the inside of the pan. **The pans should be ¾ full of batter.** Any fuller and they'll bake out. If the pans are too empty the loaves get flat. They also lose too much moisture in the baking process, producing drier loaves.

4. **Large loaves of quick bread take a long time to bake.** It's hard to be specific about baking time. Be sure the center is fully baked before removing from the oven. The loaf should be pulling away from the sides of the pan.

5. **Some of my quick bread recipes say to start out baking in a 375° oven, then back the temperature down to 350°.** Others say to bake at 350° the whole time. Experiment with both methods. See which works best for your oven.

6. **Allow quick breads to cool completely before wrapping and storing.** They keep several days at room temperature. They freeze well for future use.

7. **If your quick breads aren't tender and you are following my instructions on how to combine the ingredients, decrease the bread flour and increase the pastry flour accordingly.**

How to accurately measure flour: The bag of flour may say "sifted," but in the process of shipping it settles. To dip directly into a bag of flour will give you more flour than you need, causing dry baked goods. Use a flat or round whisk to fluff enough of the flour in the bag or canister. With a serving spoon, dip the flour into your measuring cup. A slight shake of the spoon gets the flour to fall into your cup. Make sure there are no air pockets as you are filling it. Heap the cup, then use the flat side of a knife to level it. If a recipe calls for sifted flour, sift the flour through a large strainer into a bowl. Measure same as above.

QUICK
BREADS

Sweet Potato Cornbread

MAKES: 10–12 servings

PREP. TIME: 25 minutes

BAKING TIME: 40–50 minutes

1 lb. sweet potatoes

4 large eggs

1⅓ cups buttermilk *or* plain lowfat yogurt

½ cup sugar

2 cups whole grain cornmeal

⅓ cup whole wheat bread flour

1 cup all-purpose flour

1 Tbsp. baking powder

1¼ tsp. salt

½ tsp. baking soda

¼ tsp. ground ginger, *optional*

½ cup (1 stick) chilled, unsalted butter

This very moist, slightly sweet cornbread could almost classify as a dessert.

1. Bake or microwave pierced sweet potatoes until soft. Peel. Mash. You should have a very thick mash.

2. Whisk eggs in mixing bowl. Whisk in buttermilk, sugar, and 1 packed cup mashed sweet potatoes.

3. In a large bowl, stir together cornmeal, both flours, baking powder, salt, baking soda, and optional ginger.

4. Grate chilled butter (see page 150) on top of flour mixture. Use a pastry cutter or flat whisk to cut into coarse crumbs.

5. Stir sugar up from the bottom of the egg mixture.

6. Add egg mixture to flour mixture. Stir until just blended. A few flour streaks are okay. It will continue to get mixed as you transfer it to the pan.

7. Pour into greased and floured 9" square baking dish or 10" deep-dish pie plate.

8. Bake 40–50 minutes in preheated 425°F oven until golden on top and tester comes out clean. Serve warm. Delicious served with butter and syrup or your favorite jam.

Quick Cornbread

MAKES: an 8" pan

PREP. TIME: 15 minutes

BAKING TIME: 12–15 minutes

1 Tbsp. unsalted butter

1 cup whole grain cornmeal, preferably roasted

½ cup whole wheat pastry flour

½ cup all-purpose flour

2 tsp. baking powder

½ tsp. salt

2 large eggs

1 cup whole milk

1 Tbsp. sugar

This is a Southern-style cornbread. If you prefer a sweeter Northern-style cornbread, you can increase the sugar to ¼ cup. Cut back on the milk by 2 Tbsp.

1. Preheat the oven to 425°F. Put the butter in a 8" baking pan or cast iron skillet and place it in the oven.
2. In a large bowl combine the dry ingredients.
3. In another bowl, whisk eggs, milk, and sugar until frothy.
4. Pour egg mixture over flour mixture, being sure to get all the sugar from the bottom. Stir just until barely moistened. There should be some lumps. Do not overmix!
5. Pour batter over the melted butter in the hot skillet.
6. Bake 12–15 minutes at 425°F until golden and springy in the middle. Serve hot with butter and syrup or the jam of your choice.

This recipe gets rave reviews all around. It's so moist because of all the apples.

Apple Cranberry Nut Bread

MAKES: an 8" loaf

PREP. TIME: 20 minutes

BAKING TIME: 60–65 minutes

1 cup coarsely chopped fresh *or* frozen cranberries, thawed

1 Tbsp. confectioners sugar

½ tsp. salt, *divided*

2 large eggs

¾ cup sugar

4 Tbsp butter or lard, melted

½ cup whole wheat pastry flour

½ cup whole wheat bread flour

½ cup all-purpose flour

1½ tsp. baking powder

1 tsp. ground cinnamon

½ tsp. baking soda

1 tsp. grated orange zest, *optional*

1 rounded cup diced apples, unpeeled

½ cup chopped toasted walnuts, almonds, *or* pecans, *optional*

1. Mix chopped cranberries with confectioners sugar and ¼ tsp. salt. Set aside.

2. In a mixing bowl, whisk eggs. Whisk in sugar and oil. Set aside.

3. In a large bowl, stir together flours, baking powder, cinnamon, remaining ¼ tsp. salt, baking soda, and optional orange zest.

4. Add apples and cranberry mixture. Stir briefly.

5. Stir sugar up from the bottom of the egg mixture.

6. Add the egg mixture and gently mix and fold until just combined. This is a very stiff batter.

7. Pour into parchment lined or greased and floured 8×4" loaf pan.

8. Bake 60–65 minutes in preheated 350°F oven until a toothpick inserted near the center comes out clean.

9. Cool in pan 10 minutes. Remove bread from pan to a wire rack to cool completely.

Apple Cider Spice Bread

MAKES: a 9" loaf

PREP. TIME: 25 minutes

BAKING TIME: 45–55 minutes

2 large eggs

½ cup apple cider *or* unsweetened apple juice

¼ cup plain lowfat yogurt

2 tsp. vanilla extract

½ cup brown sugar, packed

¼ cup oil

¾ cup whole wheat pastry flour

¾ cup whole wheat bread flour

½ cup all-purpose flour

2 tsp. baking powder

1 tsp. ground cinnamon

scant ½ tsp. salt

½ tsp. baking soda

½ tsp. ground nutmeg

⅓ cup chopped golden raisins

1 cup shredded, peeled tart apple, about 1 apple

1 tsp. orange zest

1. Whisk the eggs in a mixing bowl.

2. Whisk in cider, yogurt, vanilla, brown sugar, and oil. Set aside.

3. In a large bowl, stir together both flours, baking powder, cinnamon, salt, baking soda, and nutmeg.

4. Stir in raisins, apples and zest.

5. Stir sugar up from the bottom of the cider mixture.

6. Add the cider mixture to the flour mixture. Use a spatula or wooden spoon to scrape and fold just until it is combined. A few streaks of flour are fine.

7. Turn batter into a greased and floured or parchment lined 9×5" loaf pan.

8. Bake 45–55 minutes in preheated 350°F oven or until a tester comes out clean and the loaf is golden.

9. Cool 10 minutes in the pan. Remove bread to a wire rack to cool completely.

This sweet dessert bread is delicious with a cup of coffee. While I was on the phone discussing this recipe with my daughter, I overheard my grandchildren very eagerly asking for more.

Almond Poppy Seed Bread

MAKES: a 9" loaf

PREP. TIME: 15 minutes

BAKING TIME: 55–60 minutes

⅔ cup whole wheat pastry flour

⅔ cup whole wheat bread flour

⅔ cup all-purpose flour

1¼ tsp. baking powder

½ tsp. salt

2 Tbsp. poppy seeds

2 large eggs

⅔ cup oil

¾ cup whole milk

1 cup sugar

1 tsp. almond extract

1 tsp. vanilla extract

OPTIONAL GLAZE:

¼ cup confectioners sugar

2 Tbsp. orange juice *or* milk

¼ tsp. vanilla extract

⅛ tsp. almond extract

1. In a large bowl stir together flours, baking powder, salt, and poppy seeds.

2. In another bowl, whisk the eggs. Whisk in oil, milk, sugar, and both extracts.

3. Pour egg mixture over the dry ingredients.

4. Using a large flat whisk or spatula, stir and fold, scraping along the bottom of the bowl until just combined. Some streaks of flour are fine.

5. Pour batter into a greased and floured or parchment-lined 9×5" loaf pan.

6. Bake 55–60 minutes in preheated 350°F oven or until a toothpick inserted near the center comes out clean.

7. Cool in pan 10 minutes. Remove bread to cool completely on wire rack. If you wish, combine glaze ingredients and drizzle over slightly warm loaves.

Pumpkin Bread

MAKES: two 8" loaves

PREP. TIME: 20 minutes

BAKING TIME: 45–55 minutes

1 cup brown sugar, packed

1 cup sugar

2 cups thick pumpkin puree

½ cup oil

1 cup + 1 Tbsp. whole wheat pastry flour

¾ cup whole wheat bread flour

¾ cup all-purpose flour

1¼ tsp. salt

2 tsp. baking soda

1½ tsp. ground cinnamon

½ tsp. ground cloves, *optional*

½ cup chopped, toasted walnuts, *optional*

½ cup chopped raisins, *optional*

1. Combine the sugars, pumpkin and oil. Set aside.

2. In a large bowl, stir together flours, salt, baking soda, cinnamon, optional cloves, optional walnuts, and optional raisins.

3. Add pumpkin mixture to dry ingredients. Stir and fold just until moistened. Let the streaks of flour remain.

4. Pour into 2 greased or parchment-lined 8×4" baking pans.

5. Bake 45–55 minutes in preheated 350°F oven or until a tester inserted in the middle comes out clean.

6. Cool loaves in pans 10 minutes. Remove bread from the pans and cool completely on wire racks.

This Pumpkin Bread has less oil and more pumpkin than most pumpkin bread recipes.

Nearly or completely brown bananas make the best baked goods. Under-ripe bananas don't have their sugars developed. Under-ripe bananas also don't have as much nutritional value.

Extra Bananas Bread

MAKES: an 8" loaf

PREP. TIME: 30 minutes

COOKING/BAKING TIME: 70–85 minutes

5–6 very ripe bananas (about 1 lb. 8 oz., peeled)

½ cup (1 stick) unsalted butter, melted and cooled

2 large eggs, room temperature

½ cup brown sugar, packed

¼ cup sugar

1 tsp. vanilla extract

¾ cup whole wheat pastry flour

¾ cup whole wheat bread flour

¼ cup all-purpose flour

1 tsp. baking soda

½ tsp. baking powder

¼ tsp. salt

½ cup chopped, toasted walnuts or pecans

This sounds complicated, but it's delicious.

1. Place bananas in microwave-safe bowl. Cover loosely. Microwave 4–5 minutes, gently stirring bananas 2 times until bananas are soft and juices are coming out.

2. Place bananas and liquid in a strainer over a bowl. Allow to drain 15 minutes, stirring and prodding occasionally.

3. Place the banana solids in a bowl.

4. Put ½–¾ cup banana liquid in small, heavy pan. Over medium heat, stir and simmer until the liquid is thick and reduced to ¼ cup.

5. Stir reduced banana liquid back into bananas in bowl, mashing and stirring until smooth.

6. Whisk in cooled butter, eggs, both sugars, and vanilla.

7. In a large bowl, stir together the flours, baking soda, baking powder, and salt. Stir in the nuts.

8. Pour this mixture over the dry ingredients and stir, scraping up from the bottom until just moistened. Some streaks of flour are okay. It will be lumpy.

9. Turn into a greased and floured or parchment-lined 8×4" loaf pan.

10. Bake in preheated 350°F oven for 60–75 minutes or until a toothpick inserted in the middle comes out clean.

11. Cool in the pan for 10 minutes. Remove from pan to a wire rack and cool completely.

If you have a stash of overripe bananas on hand that have been in the freezer for a while, thaw them, and then drain their juice into a small, heavy kettle. Cook until reduced by half. Stir juice back into mashed bananas for concentrated flavor.

Banana Bread

MAKES: a 9" loaf

PREP. TIME: 20 minutes

BAKING TIME: 55–60 minutes

¾ cup whole wheat pastry flour

¾ cup whole wheat bread flour

½ cup all-purpose flour

1 tsp. baking powder

scant ½ tsp. salt

½ tsp. baking soda

⅓-½ cup toasted chopped walnuts *or* pecans, *optional*

3 very ripe, large bananas (1¼–1½ cups when mashed)

¼ cup plain lowfat yogurt *or* thick buttermilk, room temperature

¾ cup sugar

2 large eggs, room temperature, beaten

6 Tbsp. unsalted butter, melted and cooled

1 tsp. vanilla extract

1. In a large bowl stir together flours, baking powder, salt, and baking soda. Stir in optional nuts and set aside.

2. In another bowl, mash the bananas roughly and leave some lumps throughout.

3. Stir yogurt, sugar, beaten eggs, melted butter and vanilla into mashed banana.

4. Pour banana mixture over the dry ingredients. Use a flat whisk or spatula to stir until barely combined. The batter should be lumpy. Some streaks of flour are okay.

5. Pour into parchment-lined or greased and floured 9×5" loaf pan.

6. Bake in preheated 350°F oven for 55–60 minutes until a tester inserted in the middle comes out clean.

7. Cool in the pan for 10 minutes. Remove from pan to a wire rack and cool completely.

I included this recipe because it is quick, and you can make it if you don't have as many bananas as the recipe on page 137 calls for.

Triple Chocolate Bread

MAKES: four 3 × 5" loaves or a 9" loaf and a 3 × 5" loaf

PREP. TIME: 25 minutes

BAKING TIME: 30–50 minutes

1½ cups chocolate chips, *divided*

¾ cup whole wheat pastry flour

¾ cup whole wheat bread flour

1 cup all-purpose flour

1¼ tsp. baking powder

1 tsp. baking soda

½ tsp. salt

½ cup (1 stick) unsalted butter, room temperature

⅔ cup brown sugar, packed

2 large eggs

1½ cups unsweetened applesauce

2 tsp. vanilla extract

⅓ cup toasted walnuts *or* sliced almonds, *optional*

GLAZE:

½ cup chocolate chips

1 Tbsp. unsalted butter

2–3 Tbsp. cream, *divided*

½ cup confectioners sugar

¼ tsp. vanilla extract

pinch salt

1. Microwave 1 cup of the chocolate chips until mostly melted. Stir until completely melted. Set aside.
2. In another bowl, combine flours, baking powder, baking soda, and salt. Set aside.
3. In a large bowl, cream the butter and sugar, scraping down the sides of the bowl. Beat until light and fluffy.
4. Add eggs one at a time, beating well after each one.
5. Add the melted, cooled chocolate. Beat again.
6. Stir in applesauce and vanilla.
7. Add flour mixture to the creamed mixture and mix well, making sure to scrape around the sides and bottom of the bowl.
8. Stir in the remaining ½ cup chocolate chips and optional nuts.
9. Pour into 4 greased and floured 3×5" pans or 1 9×5" and 1 3×5".
10. Bake in preheated 350°F oven for 30–35 minutes for small pans and 50–60 minutes for large pan or until a tester inserted in the center comes out clean.
11. Cool in pans for 10 minutes. Remove from pans to a wire rack.
12. Make glaze. Melt chocolate chips and butter in small heavy saucepan. Stir in 2 Tbsp. cream. Remove from heat and stir in confectioners sugar, vanilla, and salt. Add extra cream if needed to make a thick glaze. Drizzle over warm loaves.

Orange Yogurt Bread

This is a rich sweet bread loaded with orange flavor. You could replace the orange glaze with the dark chocolate glaze from Triple Chocolate Bread (page 140) or skip the glaze altogether.

MAKES: an 8" loaf or three 3 × 5" loaves

PREP. TIME: 25 minutes

BAKING TIME: 30–65 minutes

¾ cup whole wheat pastry flour

¾ cup whole wheat bread flour

1 cup all-purpose flour

1 tsp. baking powder

½ tsp. baking soda

¼ tsp. salt

1 Tbsp. orange zest

½ cup plain lowfat yogurt

¼ cup orange juice concentrate

¼ cup water

⅔ cup unsalted butter, softened

1¼ cups sugar

2 large eggs

GLAZE:

½ cup confectioners sugar

2–3 tsp. orange juice

pinch salt

Stir in ¼ cup chopped dried cranberries or dried apricots for a variation.

1. In a bowl combine flours, baking powder, baking soda, and salt. Stir in the orange zest.

2. Separately, stir together yogurt, orange juice concentrate, and water.

3. In a large bowl, cream the butter.

4. Add sugar and cream until light and fluffy.

5. Add eggs one at a time, beating well after each addition.

6. Add ⅓ of the dry ingredients and half the orange juice mixture. Mix until just combined. Repeat. Add the remaining ⅓ of the dry ingredients and mix, scraping the sides and bottom of the bowl to make sure all is combined.

7. Pour into greased and floured or parchment-lined 8×5" loaf pan or 3 3×5" loaf pans.

8. Bake large loaf in preheated 350°F oven for 55–65 minutes and small loaves 30–35 minutes or until a tester inserted in the middle comes out clean.

9. Cool in pans for 10 minutes. Remove from pans to a wire rack.

10. Make the glaze. Stir together confectioners sugar, 2 tsp. orange juice, and salt. Add another tsp. juice if needed to get pourable yet slightly thick consistency. Drizzle over slightly warm loaves.

For chocolate zucchini bread, add:

½ cup unsweetened cocoa powder along with the dry ingredients

additional ⅓ cup sugar

I love this recipe because it really packs in the zucchini, a good thing when my zucchini plants are in top production!

Zucchini Bread

MAKES: two 8" loaves or five 3 × 5" loaves

PREP. TIME: 25 minutes

BAKING TIME: 30–65 minutes

1 cup whole wheat pastry flour

1 cup whole wheat bread flour

1¼ cups all-purpose flour

2 tsp. ground cinnamon

1 tsp. salt

2 tsp. baking soda

1 large zucchini, to yield 3 cups packed, finely shredded zucchini

1 Tbsp. lemon juice

4 large eggs

⅔ cup sugar

1 cup brown sugar, packed

1 Tbsp. vanilla extract

1 cup oil (may substitute up to ½ cup applesauce for the same amount of the oil)

½ cup chopped nuts, *optional*

⅓ cup raisins *or* dried fruit of your choice, *optional*

1. In a bowl stir together flours, cinnamon, salt, and baking soda. Set aside.
2. Cut zucchini lengthwise. Using a melon baller or spoon, scoop out and discard the seedy part. Grate finely. Place a fine sieve over a large bowl and press out ⅓–½ cup liquid. Discard liquid. Grated zucchini should weigh 1 lb. and 2 oz. Stir in the lemon juice. Set aside.
3. In a mixing bowl, whisk the eggs well until they no longer cling to the whisk.
4. Add both sugars and continue to whisk.
5. Add oil and vanilla. Continue to whisk until sugar is dissolved.
6. Stir in nuts and grated zucchini mixture.
7. Add the flour mixture and stir just until combined. Do not over stir. Some flour and zucchini lumps are okay.
8. Pour into greased and floured or parchment-lined loaf pans.
9. Bake in preheated 375°F oven for 20 minutes. Back the heat to 350°F and continue baking until toothpick inserted in center comes out clean, 10–20 minutes longer for small pans, 35–45 minutes longer for large pans.
10. Cool in pans for 10 minutes. Remove from pans to a wire rack to cool completely.
11. Wrap loaves and let set 1 day for the best flavor. Freezes well.

For added flavor, press out and discard 1 cup liquid from the grated zucchini. Add in the lemon juice and ½ cup pineapple juice, orange juice, or other flavorful juice.

For a super moist bread, skip the part where you squeeze the liquid out of the grated zucchini.

Blueberry Bread

MAKES: a 9" loaf or three 3 × 5" loaves

PREP. TIME: 20 minutes

BAKING TIME: 23–45 minutes

1 cup whole wheat bread flour

1 cup whole wheat pastry flour

½ cup all-purpose flour

1 tsp. baking powder

½ tsp. baking soda

½ tsp. salt

1⅓ cup fresh blueberries

2 large eggs, room temperature

¾ cup sugar

¼ cup orange juice concentrate, room temperature

½ cup water, room temperature

⅓ cup applesauce, room temperature

3 Tbsp. melted unsalted butter

Don't increase the amount of berries as they will sink to the bottom of the pan.

1. In a large bowl, stir together flours, baking powder, baking soda, and salt. Stir in the blueberries. Set aside.

2. In another bowl, beat the eggs. Whisk in sugar, orange juice concentrate, water, and applesauce.

3. Pour egg mixture over the dry ingredients. Using a flat whisk or spatula, stir several strokes.

4. Drizzle the melted butter over. Stir until barely combined.

5. Scrape down the sides of the bowl and stir one or 2 more strokes. The batter should be lumpy. Some streaks of flour are okay.

6. Pour batter into greased and floured or parchment-lined 9×5" loaf pan or three 3×5" loaf pans.

7. Bake in preheated 375°F oven for 15 minutes. Back the heat to 350°F and continue baking (8–12 minutes more for small pans, 20–30 minutes for 9×5") until a toothpick inserted in the center comes out clean.

8. Cool in pans for 10 minutes. Remove from pans and cool completely. Wrap tightly and allow to set 24 hours (if you can wait that long) for best flavor.

You may use frozen blueberries in this bread. Stir them into the flour mixture while they're still frozen. Before baking, allow the filled pans to stand 10–15 minutes to thaw the berries. The loaves may take longer to bake because the core temperature is lower than usual.

For more orange flavor, add more orange juice concentrate and back off accordingly on the water. You can also add grated orange zest. Don't overpower the mild flavor of the blueberries though.

1. **Technique is key to making tender scones. Work quickly and use a light touch.** It's not a perfectly neat and tidy process. You're aiming for a tender crumb. Too many stirs and pokes will overwork the dough, resulting in tough scones.

   If you prefer a scone with more body, you may work your dough more as you bring it together into a ball. This activates the gluten which gives more structure.

2. **In my recipes I use part pastry flours, part bread flours.** That yields tender hang-together scones. Each person handles dough differently. If your scones get tough, use more pastry flour and less bread flour.

3. **Use more or less whole wheat, whatever flavor and texture you prefer.** Or substitute in (Tbsp. for Tbsp.) small amounts of other whole grains for a multi-grain effect.

4. **Chilled ingredients are essential.** If the flour or any other ingredient is getting too warm, you can stop at any point and chill it. Chilling your equipment beforehand helps, too.

5. **Do not use non-fat yogurt in scones.** Full fat or at least part fat is best.

6. Most scone recipes require cutting the butter into the dry ingredients. **I find it simpler to first grate the butter (see page 150).** Work it in until it's no bigger than small peas. If the pieces are too large, the butter will bake out into pools around your scones.

7. **Always reserve some of the liquid called for so you can use it as needed.** You want to end up with a stiff, stand-up dough.

8. Use a large mixing bowl to allow room for lifting and stirring.

9. **To combine, pour your combined wet mixture over dry mixture.** Using a flexible spatula, scrape down sides, across bottom, and up through the middle. Spin the bowl and repeat. Large chunks will form and pick up the crumbs as you go. Cut through the large chunks once if necessary.

   If you need a bit more liquid to get the dry crumbs to come together, **drizzle in just a few drops at a time** to bring the dough together into large pieces with a minimal amount of crumbs left at the bottom. Roll the chunks of dough around to pick up the last crumbs. A few floury spots are okay.

10. **If your dough gets too wet to form scones, you can make drop scones.**

    Sprinkle your work surface lightly with wheat bran (for nuttiness) or flour. Turn your chunks of dough onto the prepared work surface. Most recipes tell you to knead the dough a few strokes. This is not kneading as in bread strokes. It is more like folding to bring the dough together. Use your hands and a bench scraper to pat and form the dough into a 1"-thick round. Cut into wedges.

11. **For small scones, square the dough into a 1"-thick rectangle.** Cut lengthwise down the center, then cut small wedges zigzag style along each length of dough. Use a floured bench scraper to quickly swipe each one off the counter surface. Then place 2" apart on parchment-lined baking sheet.

12. **For layered scones, turn the chunks of dough onto a lightly floured surface.** (Save some bran to toss underneath the dough after your last fold.) Press and flatten the dough into a rectangle roughly 8" × 12". Visually divide, or lightly score, the dough into thirds.

If you want to add a thin layer of spread (nut butter, jam, curd, etc.) spread it on the two **outer** thirds of the dough.

Using a quick swipe with your bench scraper, lift and fold just as you would fold a piece of paper into thirds. You're not working for neat and tidy at this point. Repeat if you want. Toss reserved bran underneath if possible.

13. For large scones, cut into wedges. For small scones, cut as described in Tip 12 above.

14. Scones need 10 minutes rest time **after** you've shaped them and **before** they go into the oven to bake. So preheat your oven whenever appropriate in the process, so the scones get their 10-minute rest. This allows time to break up any gluten strands that may have started to form in the mixing process.

15. **Just before putting the scones into the oven,** brush the tops with cream or milk and sprinkle with coarse sugar or whatever topping you choose.

16. **Scones should be baked on the top or second to top rack of a moderately hot 375–400° F oven.** It really depends on the speed of your oven. If the scones are browning before they are fully baked, cover them with foil and/or decrease your oven temp a bit.

17. **You can freeze formed scones if you're going to bake them up to one week later.** After they're frozen, peel them from the parchment paper and place them in a heavy freezer bag. One hour before baking, place them on a parchment-lined baking sheet to thaw. Bake as instructed. They may take extra baking time if they're still chilled in the center.

18. **I like to prep scones before I need them.** After I've cut the butter into the dry ingredients, I cover the bowl tightly and refrigerate it. I pre-mix the wet ingredients, put them in a jar, and refrigerate them. Then everything is ready to assemble and bake when I want to make them within the next day or two. **Remember to stir your wet ingredients up from the bottom before pouring them over the dry ingredients.**

To grate butter, take a stick of cold butter: hold the end. Peel the paper back over your fingers. Using the paper end as a handle, grate the butter on a flat hand held medium hole grater held level 4 inches above the flour mixture. Let the grated butter fall straight down into the combined dry ingredients. Stop occasionally. Use a fork to toss the butter into the flour mixture and toss the flour mixture over the front and back of the grater. Continue grating the desired amount of butter from the stick. Toss the flour and the shreds of butter until they are all coated and mixed throughout. Using a flexible flat whisk or two table knives, cut throughout the mixture, tossing and cutting until the butter pieces are the required size for your recipe.

If the stick of butter gets melty in your hand before you are finished grating, check how much you grated off the stick and put that stick back into the refrigerator. Get another cold stick and grate the remainder.

SCONES

These scones are a down-home, hearty scone with a full oat flavor. They're great on their own, but variations are good too.

Oatmeal Scones

MAKES: 8 scones

PREP. TIME: 30 minutes

BAKING TIME: 17–25 minutes

1½ cups rolled oats, *divided*

1 large egg, cold

⅓ cup + 1 Tbsp. sugar, *divided*

½ tsp. vanilla extract

½ cup cream *or* half-and-half, cold, *divided*

½ cup whole wheat pastry flour

½ cup whole wheat bread flour

2½ tsp. baking powder

¼ tsp. salt

½ cup (1 stick) cold, unsalted butter

1 Tbsp. wheat bran

VARIATION 1:

Toast ½ cup chopped pecans. Cool. Stir into the flour mixture in Step 4. Add ½ tsp. maple extract/flavoring in Step 3. Omit the sugar sprinkle in Step 13. When cooled, glaze with 1½ Tbsp. maple syrup whisked into 6 Tbsp. confectioners sugar.

1. Spread the oats on a rimmed baking sheet. Toast at 375°F, stirring frequently until fragrant and a bit golden, 7–9 minutes. Cool completely. Set aside ½ cup + 2 Tbsp. toasted oats.

2. Place remaining toasted oats in food processor or blender. Process to the texture of coarse flour. Now you've made oat flour.

3. In a small bowl, whisk the egg and stir in ⅓ cup sugar, vanilla, and 6 Tbsp. cream.

4. In a large bowl, stir together flours, oat flour, baking powder, and salt.

5. Grate the cold butter (see page 150) on top of the flour mixture. Use a flat whisk to cut it further into the flour until the size of small pefas.

6. Stir in the reserved ½ cup toasted oats.

7. Stir any undissolved sugar up from the bottom of the egg mixture.

8. Add the egg mixture. Use a rubber spatula to scrape down the sides, across the bottom, and up through the middle. Repeat until large chunks of dough form. Cut once through the chunks. There should be a minimal amount of crumbs left on the bottom of the bowl. Drizzle up to 2 Tbsp. reserved cream if needed to pick them up in the dough.

9. Sprinkle the work surface with 1 Tbsp. wheat bran and 1 Tbsp. reserved oats.

10. Turn dough out onto the sprinkled surface. Sprinkle the remaining 1 Tbsp. oats on the dough.

11. Pat dough into a 1"-thick circle.

12. Cut desired size pieces with floured bench scraper. Use a quick motion to scrape each scone from the work surface and place them 2" apart on parchment-lined baking sheets.

13. Brush tops with cream and sprinkle with remaining 1 Tbsp. sugar.

14. Bake in preheated 400°F oven for 10–15 minutes on the top rack of the oven until golden and springy when touched. Allow to cool 5 minutes on baking sheets, and then slide onto wire racks.

VARIATION 2:

Toast ½ cup almonds. Chop dried apricots to make ½ cup. Stir both in when you stir in the oats in Step 6. Omit the sugar sprinkle in Step 13. When cooled, glaze with a mixture of 6 Tbsp. confectioners sugar and a miniscule pinch of salt, thinned with a bit of whole milk.

S avor the flavors of the sharp cheese and apple pared with the nuttiness of whole wheat.

Apple Cheddar Scones

MAKES: 8 scones

PREP. TIME: 25 minutes

BAKING TIME: 10–15 minutes

½ cup whole wheat pastry flour

½ cup whole wheat bread flour

1 cup all-purpose flour

2 Tbsp. sugar

3 tsp. baking powder

¼ tsp. salt

¼ tsp. baking soda

5 Tbsp. cold, unsalted butter

1 cup shredded extra-sharp cheddar cheese, loosely packed

1 cup finely chopped *or* grated apple, loosely packed

¾ cup plain yogurt *or* thick buttermilk, cold

1. In a large bowl combine flours, sugar, baking powder, salt, and baking soda.

2. Grate the cold butter (see page 150) on top of the flour mixture. Use a flat whisk to cut it further into the flour until the size of small peas.

3. Stir in cheese and apples.

4. Add the yogurt or buttermilk. Use a rubber spatula to scrape down the sides, across the bottom, and up through the middle. Repeat until large chunks of dough form. Cut once through the chunks. There should be a minimal amount of crumbs left on the bottom of the bowl. Drizzle in a few more drops of yogurt if needed to pick them up in the dough.

5. Sprinkle work surface with wheat bran and/or whole wheat bread flour. Turn dough onto prepared surface. Pat dough into a 1"-thick circle.

6. Cut desired size pieces with floured bench scraper. Use a quick motion to scrape each scone from the work surface and place them 2" apart on parchment-lined baking sheets.

7. Brush tops with cream.

8. Bake in preheated 400°F oven for 10–15 minutes on the top rack of the oven until golden and springy when touched. Allow to cool 5 minutes on baking sheets, and then slide onto wire racks.

Orange Anise Drop Scones

These are tender and flavorful, almost like a cookie.

MAKES: 8 scones

PREP. TIME: 25 minutes

BAKING TIME: 8–12 minutes

1 Tbsp. orange zest

⅓ cup sugar

2 tsp. anise seed *

½ cup whole wheat pastry flour

½ cup whole wheat bread flour

¼ cup all-purpose flour

1½ tsp. baking powder

¼ tsp. baking soda

¼ tsp. salt

4 Tbsp. (half stick) cold, unsalted butter

¼ cup coarsely chopped golden raisins

1 large egg, cold

6 Tbsp. sour cream *or* Greek yogurt, kept cold

1 tsp. vanilla extract

* *Omit the anise if you don't care for its licorice-y flavor.*

1. Process the zest, sugar, and anise seed in a food processor until combined. Set aside 1½ tsp. for sprinkling on tops.

2. In a large bowl (chilled is best), combine the flours, baking powder, baking soda, salt, and remaining sugar/anise mixture.

3. Grate the cold butter (see page 150) on top of the flour mixture. Use a flat whisk to cut it further into the flour until pea-size. Use your hands to rub it between your fingers a bit until like coarse cornmeal.

4. Stir in the golden raisins.

5. In a small bowl, whisk the egg. Whisk in the sour cream and vanilla.

6. Add egg mixture to dry ingredients. Use a rubber spatula to scrape down the sides, across the bottom, and up through the middle. Repeat until large chunks of dough form. Cut once through the chunks. There should be a minimal amount of crumbs left on the bottom of the bowl. Drizzle a few drops of sour cream if needed to pick them up in the dough.

7. Drop 8 even dollops 2″ apart onto a parchment-lined baking sheet.

8. Sprinkle with remaining sugar mixture.

9. Bake in preheated 400°F oven for 8–12 minutes on top rack of oven until light and springy. Allow to cool 5 minutes on baking sheets, and then slide onto wire racks.

Lemon Yogurt Scones

MAKES: 8 scones

PREP. TIME: 25 minutes

BAKING TIME: 10–15 minutes

⅔ cup plain yogurt *or* thick buttermilk

5 Tbsp. sugar, *divided*

⅔ cup whole wheat bread flour

⅔ cup whole wheat pastry flour

⅔ cup all-purpose flour

2 tsp. baking powder

¼ tsp. baking soda

¼ tsp. salt

2 tsp. lemon zest,* *divided*

⅓–½ cup chopped golden raisins *or* dried apricots, *optional*

⅓ cup cold, unsalted butter

cream *or* milk for brushing tops

* *More or less lemon is okay.*

1. Whisk together yogurt and 3 Tbsp. sugar. Set aside.

2. In a large bowl combine flours, baking powder, baking soda, salt, and 1½ tsp. lemon zest.

3. Grate the cold butter (see page 150) on top of the flour mixture. Use a flat whisk to cut it further into the flour until the size of small peas.

4. Stir in the optional chopped fruit.

5. Stir yogurt mixture again to get any undissolved sugar up off the bottom.

6. Add yogurt mixture to flour mixture. Use a rubber spatula to scrape down the sides, across the bottom, and up through the middle. Repeat until large chunks of dough form. Cut once through the chunks. There should be a minimal amount of crumbs left on the bottom of the bowl. Drizzle in a few more drops of yogurt if needed to pick them up in the dough.

7. Sprinkle work surface with wheat bran or whole wheat bread flour. Turn dough onto prepared surface. Pat into a 1"-thick circle.

8. Cut desired size pieces with floured bench scraper. Use a quick motion to scrape each scone from the work surface and place them 2" apart on parchment-lined baking sheets.

9. Brush tops with cream.

10. Combine the remaining 2 Tbsp. sugar and remaining ½ tsp. lemon zest until texture of damp sand. Sprinkle lemon sugar over tops of scones.

11. Bake in preheated 400°F oven for 10–15 minutes on the top rack of the oven until golden and springy when touched. Allow to cool 5 minutes on baking sheets, and then slide onto wire racks.

Blueberry Scones

MAKES: 12–16 scones

PREP. TIME: 25 minutes

BAKING TIME: 10–15 minutes

½ cup heavy cream

½ cup thick buttermilk *or*
plain yogurt, 2 Tbsp.
reserved

½ cup + 1 Tbsp. sugar,
divided

1¼ cups whole wheat
pastry flour

1 cup whole wheat bread
flour

1 cup all-purpose flour

3½ tsp. baking powder

½ tsp. baking soda

½ tsp. salt

1–2 tsp. finely grated
lemon zest, *optional*

12 Tbsp. (¾ cup) cold,
unsalted butter

1¼ cups fresh *or* frozen
blueberries, barely
thawed

*If you don't
have any
buttermilk
or yogurt on
hand, use
milk and
omit the
baking soda.*

1. Whisk together cream, buttermilk,
and ½ cup sugar. Set aside.

2. In a large bowl, combine flours,
baking powder, baking soda, salt,
and optional zest.

3. Grate the cold butter (see page
150) on top of the flour mixture. Use
a flat whisk to cut it further into the
flour until the size of small peas.

4. Gently stir in the blueberries.

5. Whisk the cream mixture again to
get any undissolved sugar up off the bottom.

6. Pour cream mixture over dry ingredients. Use a rubber
spatula to scrape down the sides, across the bottom, and
up through the middle. Repeat until large chunks of dough
form. Cut once through the chunks. There should be a
minimal amount of crumbs left on the bottom of the bowl.
Drizzle in the reserved cream if needed to pick them up in
the dough.

7. Sprinkle work surface with wheat bran or whole wheat
bread flour. Turn dough onto prepared surface. Divide in
half. Pat into a two 1"-thick circles.

8. Cut desired size pieces with floured bench scraper. Use a
quick motion to scrape each scone from the work surface
and place them 2" apart on parchment-lined baking sheets.

9. Brush tops with cream. Sprinkle with reserved 1 Tbsp.
sugar or, if you prefer, lemon sugar (see Step 10 of Lemon
Yogurt Scones page 159).

10. Bake in preheated 400°F oven for 10–15 minutes on the
top rack of the oven until golden and springy when touched.
Allow to cool 5 minutes on baking sheets, and then slide
onto wire racks.

*You can halve
the recipe but
it really is so
delicious you
will want
to make the
full batch
and freeze
the extras
for a quick
breakfast or
coffee break.*

One time when I made these, I used 1¼ cups chopped frozen unsweetened strawberries. I put them in a strainer over a bowl and thawed them nearly the whole way. I ended up with about ¾ cup of rather mushy strawberries but it was plenty. The flavor and intensity of home frozen strawberries is delicious. I put the juice that drained from them back into the freezer and used it in another dessert.

Strawberry Scones

MAKES: 8–12 scones

PREP. TIME: 25 minutes

BAKING TIME: 10–15 minutes

1 large egg, cold

¼ cup light cream, cold

⅓ cup sugar

½ tsp. vanilla extract, *optional*

¾ cup whole wheat pastry flour

¾ cup whole wheat bread flour

½ cup all-purpose flour

1 Tbsp. baking powder

¼ tsp. baking soda

zest of 1 lemon, *optional*

5 Tbsp. cold, unsalted butter

1 cup hulled, finely diced strawberries, chilled

1 Tbsp. coarse sugar

1. Whisk the egg. Whisk in the cream, sugar and optional vanilla. Chill.

2. In a large bowl stir together flours, baking powder, and baking soda. Stir in the optional lemon zest.

3. Grate the cold butter (see page 150) on top of the flour mixture. Use a flat whisk to cut it further into the flour until the size of small peas.

4. Add the strawberries. Gently toss into flour mixture.

5. Stir the chilled cream mixture to lift any undissolved sugar up from the bottom. Pour over the flour mixture.

6. Use a rubber spatula to scrape down the sides, across the bottom, and up through the middle. Repeat until large chunks of dough form. Cut once through the chunks if needed. Drizzle in the reserved cream a few drops at a time as needed to bring the dough together. Roll the chunks to pick up the remaining crumbs.

7. Sprinkle work surface with wheat bran or flour. Turn dough onto prepared surface. Pat into a 1"-thick circle or rectangle.

8. Cut desired size pieces with floured bench scraper. Use a quick motion to scrape each scone from the work surface and place them 2" apart on parchment-lined baking sheets.

9. Brush with cream and sprinkle with coarse sugar.

10. Bake on the top rack in preheated 400°F oven for 10–15 minutes, or until golden and spongy when touched. Slide onto wire rack to cool.

You can add a pinch of nutmeg if you like. Go easy, though. You don't want to overpower the delicate flavor of the strawberries.

Cranberry Orange Scones

MAKES: 8 scones

PREP. TIME: 25 minutes

BAKING TIME: 10–15 minutes

1 cup cranberries, fresh or partially frozen *

¼ tsp. salt, *divided*

2 tsp. confectioners sugar

½ cup + 2 Tbsp. all-purpose flour

½ cup whole wheat pastry flour

½ cup whole wheat bread flour

2½ tsp. baking powder

¼ tsp. baking soda

5 Tbsp. cold, unsalted butter

1 tsp. finely grated orange zest

½ cup plain yogurt *or* thick buttermilk, reserve 2 Tbsp.

4 Tbsp. sugar, *divided*

2 Tbsp. frozen orange juice concentrate *or* milk

* *If you don't have fresh or frozen cranberries, use ½–⅔ cup chopped dried cranberries and add them along with the orange zest in Step 4.*

For more cranberry flavor add an extra 3 Tbsp. chopped dried cranberries. Stir in with the orange zest in Step 4.

1. Chop cranberries. Stir in ⅛ tsp. salt and confectioners sugar. Set aside to macerate.

2. In a large bowl, combine flours, baking powder, baking soda, and ⅛ tsp. salt.

3. Grate the cold butter (see page 150) on top of the flour mixture. Use a flat whisk to cut it further into the flour until the size of small peas.

4. Add and stir in the chopped cranberry mixture and orange zest.

5. Stir together yogurt, 3 Tbsp. sugar, and orange juice concentrate.

6. Add yogurt mixture to flour mixture. Scrape out any undissolved sugar on the bottom. Use a rubber spatula to scrape down the sides, across the bottom, and up through the middle. Repeat until large chunks of dough form. Cut once through the chunks. There should be a minimal amount of crumbs left on the bottom of the bowl. Drizzle in the reserved yogurt if needed to pick them up in the stiff dough.

7. Sprinkle work surface with wheat bran or whole wheat bread flour. Turn dough onto prepared surface. Pat dough into a 1"-thick circle.

8. Cut desired size pieces with floured bench scraper. Use a quick motion to scrape each scone from the work surface and place them 2" apart on parchment-lined baking sheets.

9. Brush tops with cream. Sprinkle with reserved 1 Tbsp. sugar.

10. Bake in preheated 400°F oven for 10–15 minutes on the top rack of the oven until golden and springy when touched. Allow to cool 5 minutes on baking sheets, and then slide onto wire racks.

*C*ream scones are so nearly perfect that I wasn't sure I should try to convert them to being whole grain. But I couldn't resist, and tried them on a group of people I had over for a breakfast. For the most part, these people are not fans of whole grains. But they said these were the best scones they ever ate!

Cream Scones

MAKES: 8 scones

PREP. TIME: 25 minutes

BAKING TIME: 10–15 minutes

½ cup whole wheat pastry flour

½ cup whole wheat bread flour

1 cup + 2 Tbsp. all-purpose flour

1 Tbsp. baking powder

2–4 Tbsp. sugar, according to your taste preference

¼ tsp. salt

5 Tbsp. cold, unsalted butter

½ cup finely chopped raisins (may use 1–2 tsp. flour to chop them with, *optional*)

¾–1 cup heavy cream

1 Tbsp. coarse sugar

1. In a large bowl stir together flours, baking powder, sugar, and salt.

2. Grate the cold butter (see page 150) on top of the flour mixture. Use a flat whisk to cut it further into the flour until the size of small peas.

3. Stir in the chopped raisins.

4. Pour ¾ cup cream over dry ingredients. Use a rubber spatula to scrape down the sides, across the bottom, and up through the middle. Repeat until large chunks of dough form. Cut once through the chunks. There should be a minimal amount of crumbs left on the bottom of the bowl. Drizzle in more cream, 1 Tbsp. at a time, to pick them up in the dough. The dough should be stiff.

5. Turn dough onto clean work surface. Pat into a 7×10" rectangle. Lifting with a bench scraper, fold dough into thirds as you would fold a piece of paper for a business letter. Repeat patting and folding.

6. Pat dough into a 1"-thick circle.

7. Cut desired size pieces with floured bench scraper. Use a quick motion to scrape each scone from the work surface and place them 2" apart on parchment-lined baking sheets.

8. Brush tops with cream. Sprinkle with coarse sugar.

9. Bake in preheated 400°F oven for 10–15 minutes on the top rack of the oven until golden and springy when touched. Allow to cool 5 minutes on baking sheets, and then slide onto wire racks.

Double Chocolate Scones

MAKES: 8–12 scones

PREP. TIME: 30 minutes

COOLING TIME: 30–40 minutes

BAKING TIME: 8–10 minutes

¼ cup heavy cream

⅔ cup Ghiradelli 60%-cacao bittersweet chocolate chips, *divided*

5 Tbsp. + 1 tsp. cold unsalted butter, *divided*

½ cup whole wheat bread flour

½ cup + 2 Tbsp. whole wheat pastry flour

1 cup all-purpose flour

1 Tbsp. baking powder

2–3 Tbsp. sugar, according to your taste preference

½ tsp. salt

¼ cup chopped walnuts, *optional*

⅔ cup light cream *or* whole milk, and maybe a little more

coarse sugar, *optional*

1. Make a ganache: In a 1-cup glass measure in the microwave or small pan on the stovetop, bring the cream just to a boil. Watch closely. Place ⅓ cup chocolate chips in a mug or small glass bowl. Pour the boiling cream over. Let set 2 minutes. Add 1 tsp. butter and whisk until satiny. Set aside for 15–20 minutes to cool to room temperature. Do not refrigerate or the ganache will become hard and grainy.

2. In a large bowl stir together flours, baking powder, sugar, and salt.

3. Grate the 5 Tbsp. cold butter (see page 150) on top of the flour mixture. Use a flat whisk to cut it further into the flour until the size of small peas.

4. Stir in the remaining ⅓ cup chocolate chips and optional nuts.

5. If the ganache is not cooled to room temperature, refrigerate the flour mixture while you wait.

6. Add approximately 3 Tbsp. ganache to ⅔ cup light cream. Whisk together. It will appear a bit grainy.

7. Pour light cream/ganache mixture over flour mixture. Use a rubber spatula to scrape down the sides, across the bottom, and up through the middle. Repeat until large chunks of dough form. Cut once through the chunks. There should be a minimal amount of crumbs left on the bottom of the bowl. Drizzle in a little more cream if needed to pick them up in the stiff dough.

8. Turn dough onto clean work surface. Pat into a 7×10″ rectangle.

9. Spread half of the remaining ganache over the 2 outer thirds of the rectangle. Leave the middle third empty.

10. Use a bench scraper to lift a third of the rectangle spread with ganache, folding it into the middle and then folding the other third spread with ganache over it, just as you would fold a piece of paper for a business letter. Repeat the patting, spreading, and folding. This can get a bit messy, but be assured that it's worth it!

11. Pat the ganache-layered, folded dough down to a 1″ thick rectangle.

12. Use a floured bench scraper to cut evenly into wedges. Place wedges 2" apart on a parchment-lined baking pan.

13. Brush tops with cream. Sprinkle with coarse sugar if desired.

14. Bake in preheated 400°F oven for 8–10 minutes on the top rack of the oven until golden and springy when touched. The tops may slide a bit during baking but the delicious taste is worth the irregular appearance.

15. Allow to cool 5 minutes on baking sheets, and then slide onto wire racks. Allow to cool a further 10–20 minutes before serving.

As a variation, omit the green onions and add instead:

1 clove garlic minced (¼ tsp. dried)

½ cup chopped fresh (2½ Tbsp. dried) basil

This gives the scones a pizza flavor.

Tomato Feta Scones

MAKES: 8 scones

PREP. TIME: 25 minutes

BAKING TIME: 10–15 minutes

1¼ cups whole wheat pastry flour

¾ cup all-purpose flour

2 tsp. baking powder

½ tsp. baking soda

2 tsp. sugar

4 Tbsp. (half stick) cold, unsalted butter

½ cup crumbled feta cheese

½ cup chopped green onions

½ cup coarsely chopped, reconstituted sun-dried tomatoes *

⅓ cup chopped, toasted walnuts, *optional*

½ cup thick buttermilk *or* plain lowfat yogurt, cold, 2 Tbsp. reserved

1 large egg, cold

* RECONSTITUTING SUN-DRIED TOMATOES:

1. Place desired amount of tomatoes in a glass bowl.
2. Pour boiling water over to cover completely. Let set 20–30 minutes.
3. Drain, reserving juice for soup or gravy.
4. Cool tomatoes completely and chop as desired.
5. Any extra drained tomatoes can be placed in a small jar with a tight-fitting lid. Cover completely with extra-virgin olive oil. Store in the refrigerator. As you use the tomatoes, save the flavored oil to use in dressings and marinades.

1. In a large bowl, stir together flours, baking powder, baking soda, and sugar.

2. Grate the cold butter (see page 150) on top of the flour mixture. Use a flat whisk to cut it further into the flour until the size of small peas.

3. Add cheese, onions, tomatoes, and optional walnuts. Toss with a fork.

4. Beat egg in a small bowl. Add buttermilk and stir.

5. Pour egg mixture over flour mixture. Use a rubber spatula to scrape down the sides, across the bottom, and up through the middle. Repeat until large chunks of dough form. Cut once through the chunks. There should be a minimal amount of crumbs left on the bottom of the bowl. Drizzle in a little reserved buttermilk if needed to pick them up in the dough. The dough should be stiff.

6. Sprinkle work surface with wheat bran or whole wheat bread flour. Turn dough onto prepared surface. Pat dough into a 1"-thick circle.

7. Cut desired size pieces with floured bench scraper. Use a quick motion to scrape each scone from the work surface and place them 2" apart on parchment-lined baking sheets.

8. Bake in preheated 400°F oven for 10–15 minutes on the top rack of the oven until golden and springy when touched. Allow to cool 5 minutes on baking sheets, and then slide onto wire racks. Serve warm, almost a meal in themselves, or serve with soup or salad.

Spinach Feta Scones

MAKES: 8 scones

PREP. TIME: 25 minutes

BAKING TIME: 10–15 minutes

1¼ cups whole wheat pastry
  flour

¾ cup all-purpose flour

2 tsp. baking powder

½ tsp. baking soda

2 tsp. sugar

¼ tsp. granulated garlic

4 Tbsp. (half stick) cold,
  unsalted butter

½ cup crumbled feta cheese

2 Tbsp. finely chopped onion

5 oz. (about ½ cup) steamed,
  well-drained, finely
  chopped spinach, coarse
  ribs removed, chilled

dash red pepper flakes,
  optional

½ cup cold thick buttermilk
  or plain lowfat yogurt, 2
  Tbsp. reserved

1 large egg, cold

1. In a large bowl stir together flours, baking powder, baking soda, sugar, and garlic.

2. Grate the cold butter (see page 150) on top of the flour mixture. Use a flat whisk to cut it further into the flour until the size of small peas.

3. Add the cheese, onion, chilled spinach, and optional pepper flakes. Toss together with a fork to evenly distribute the spinach.

4. Combine the buttermilk and beaten egg. Pour over the dry ingredients.

5. Use a rubber spatula to scrape down the sides, across the bottom, and up through the middle. Repeat until large chunks of dough form. Cut once through the chunks. There should be a minimal amount of crumbs left on the bottom of the bowl. Drizzle in a little reserved buttermilk if needed to pick them up in the dough.

6. Sprinkle work surface with wheat bran or whole wheat bread flour. Turn dough onto prepared surface. Pat dough into a 1"-thick circle.

7. Cut desired size pieces with floured bench scraper. Use a quick motion to scrape each scone from the work surface and place them 2" apart on parchment-lined baking sheets.

8. Bake in preheated 400°F oven for 10–15 minutes on the top rack of the oven until golden and springy when touched. Allow to cool 5 minutes on baking sheets, and then slide onto wire racks. Delicious spread with butter or basil pesto (see page 64).

Tips and Tricks for Making Yeast Breads

1. **You can purchase yeast in bulk or in individual packages.** For the occasional bread baker, buy individual packages as needed. Use one individual package of yeast when your recipe calls for 1 Tbsp. of yeast.

If you have yeast on hand and you're not sure that it's still viable, proof-test it. Whisk together in a warmed liquid measuring cup ¼ cup warm water (110–115° F), 1 tsp. sugar, and 1 Tbsp. yeast. If everything is warm enough, the yeast should be foaming within 5 minutes.

Store yeast tightly sealed in a cool, dark, dry place.

2. **For the liquid in bread dough, use water, milk (pasteurized or raw), pasta cooking water, or potato cooking water.** If there was salt added to the liquid, reduce the amount of salt that you add to the dough accordingly.

Raw milk, no matter how fresh, pasta cooking water (use sparingly, it's very starchy), and potato water must all be heated to 180° and cooled before using. Enzymes that inhibit yeast activity form quickly.

To scald milk, measure out a bit more than you need into a heavy-bottom kettle. The smaller the surface area, the better, so that you get less skin. Heat the milk to 180°, or until tiny bubbles form over the surface. Watch closely that it doesn't boil over. Remove from the heat. Once cooled, pour it off into the liquid measure, leaving the skin behind (the skin inhibits bread rise). You may need to add water to make up the difference that was lost in evaporation. Or scald your milk in the microwave. Stir occasionally and watch closely.

Buttermilk, acid whey, or tomato juice (for pink bread) also can be used as the liquid in bread. Raw buttermilk must be scalded. Don't worry if it curdles. Whisk or blend it to break up the curd. Add ¼ tsp. baking soda per 1½ cups liquid to neutralize the acidity of these liquids.

Sweet whey from yogurt or other cultured cheeses work, too. (And because the acidity is mild in sweet whey, there's no need to neutralize it with baking soda.)

3. **Milk-based breads bake up softer and have a brown crust; water-based breads are not as soft and much paler.**

4. **The sweetener (honey, maple syrup, molasses, raw sugar, sugar, brown sugar) that you use in your bread is a matter of personal taste.** Liquid sweeteners add extra liquid. If using ¼ cup honey in place of ¼ cup sugar, decrease the other added liquid by 1 Tbsp.

5. **Adding live vinegar (preferably the non-distilled Braggs brand or your own homemade) to bread dough helps to extend the shelf life of the bread.** It's a cheap dough

conditioner, although many people say that it flattens the flavor of bread. I usually add vinegar only to my everyday, all whole-grain bread dough: 1 tsp. per 3 cups flour. You don't

taste it.

To boost the rise and texture of your bread, add a pinch of baking soda along with the vinegar. If your bread flour is enriched, you can skip the vinegar, because enriched flour already contains dough conditioners.

6. **Ingredients and equipment must be warmed to room temperature.** Adding warm liquid into a cold bowl will chill it and result in lazy yeast. Cold flour, eggs, etc. will do the same. Warm your large bowl. A bit of hot water or 8–10 seconds inverted over an open gas flame works well.

7. **Always begin by using the lesser amount of flour called for in a recipe.** Add in the rest as needed to make a workable dough. If you consistently need to add more than the full amount, check your measuring cups for accuracy. Air humidity also plays a part in the dough's stickiness.

8. **How to knead bread.** After you've brought the dough together into a workable ball, turn it onto the work surface and knead it according to the recipe's instructions. Now is your chance to be aggressive with your dough. The kneading motion is as much a full body motion as it is a technique of the hands. Get your whole body into the swing of it.

Firmly push into the dough, bearing down with the heels of your hands as you push it away from your body. Spin it ¼ turn and fold it as you are sliding it back toward yourself. Push, spin ¼ turn, fold, pull back. Repeat this motion until the dough is smooth and elastic.

To prevent sticking, keep the remaining white flour at the far side of the counter so you can pick up a tiny dusting on the smooth side of the dough each time you push the dough away. Never sprinkle the flour on top of the dough.

9. **For loaves that you want to slice, you'll need a firmer dough that's been kneaded up to 15 minutes to develop elasticity.**

10. **For a rich sweet dough, or a dough that doesn't need a fine texture, knead for only 3–5 minutes.** Rich dough should be worked as sticky as possible. Use a bench scraper to assist with lifting and folding sticky dough. It's frustrating until you get the feel for it, but tender baked goods are unbeatable.

11. **To grease the bowl where the bread will rise, put a puddle of oil that's one inch round in the bottom of the unwashed bowl that you've used for mixing the dough.** Tip it to get the oil to go up the sides here and there. Add your kneaded dough, smooth side down. Spin and twirl the dough up the sides of the bowl. Then flip the dough greased side up. Cover.

12. **Your "dampened towel" should either be linen or a soft non-terry cotton.** Dampen lightly. Too wet and it will stick to your dough. If sticking is a problem, place a dry towel underneath the damp one. Never rewet it for the second rise. You can use plastic wrap in place of a damp towel.

13. **If you set your dough to rise in the direct path of an HVAC vent it will get a dry crust on top, preventing it from rising properly.** Your oven is a warm, draft-free place to set your dough to rise.

Before starting to assemble your dough, turn your oven to the lowest temperature, 170°F. Turn off the heat as soon as it comes to temperature. When you're finished kneading the dough, the oven temp should be perfect.

You can warm the bowl in the oven at the same time. Take it out before it gets too hot. If your kneaded bread dough seems dry, place a pan of warm water on the bottom rack of the oven to boost the warmth and moisture. I do not recommend this for sticky dough.

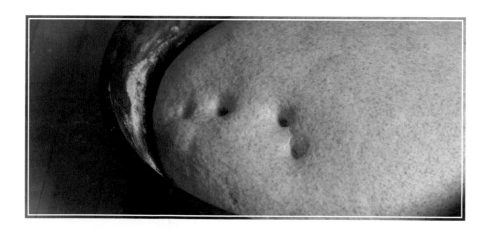

14. **After the dough has risen, handle your dough gently as you form it into the shape you want.**

15. **A bench scraper is a bread baker's best friend. As you are forming the risen dough, it's better for it to stick to your work surface than to add in extra flour.** However, a quick toss of flour on the outside of the already formed bread is sometimes necessary to get it from the work surface to the baking pan.

16. **"Nearly double" means just that. If you let formed loaves rise too long, they'll become loose and crumbly in the middle.**

17. **"Oven spring" is the rising that takes place during the first minutes of baking until the yeast is no longer active.** Yeast forms gases that are trapped in tiny pockets in bread dough. This is what makes the bread rise. If the top surface of your bread has a thin, dry crust when it goes into the oven, the gases are prevented from further expanding during the early part of baking

18. To promote oven spring, before you put your fancy braids or rolls in the oven to bake:
    - Brush with melted butter or oil for a soft top crust.
    - Brush with beaten egg or egg white for a shiny golden surface and to help seeds and nuts to adhere.

19. **To promote oven spring in everyday loaves baked in bread pans, you can brush them in one of the above ways and/or:**
    - Immediately before baking, use a sharp knife or razor blade to slash just the surface. Create either one long slash down the center or several evenly spaced diagonal slashes.
    - Immediately before baking, pierce the top of the loaf with a sharp-tined fork several times. The dough will slightly deflate around the holes, but it won't harm the loaf.

20. **To test if a loaf is done, run a knife blade around the loaf.** Carefully slide it out of the pan onto its side. Using the handle of a table knife, rap sharply on the bottom of the loaf. If it sounds quite hollow, it's done. If you have to imagine that it sounds hollow, place it back in the hot pan and bake 5 minutes longer.

    For rolls baked on a metal baking pan, use the handle of a table knife to rap the bottom of the pan. Or you can cheat and lift the top crust of a center roll just enough to see if it's no longer doughy.

21. **Heat escapes each time you open the oven door.** It's best not to open the oven door until your bread is finished.

22. If your loaves of bread consistently have large holes in them, your oven may have too wide a variance in temperature. If you have been using convection bake, try using regular bake. If you are using regular bake, the temperature regulator may not be functioning properly. Be sure that your oven vent isn't blocked. You should feel heat and some steam coming out of the vent as the bread bakes.

23. After the loaves are completely cooled, put them in plastic bags for 1 hour or so. This softens the crust, making it easier to slice.

24. Well-seasoned loaf pans are a pleasure to use. I use my glass loaf pans only for baking bread. I never scrub them with detergent. Scrape off anything that is stuck and wipe with a dry cloth.

To season your pans, grease very heavily before placing the loaves in them to rise. You will have to do this several times before the seasoning is built up. Over time, back off on the amount of greasing. Once seasoned, just a light amount of greasing is enough. For the occasional baker, bag and store your seasoned pans in the freezer so they don't become rancid.

25. If you need to use your bread pans for baking quick breads, meat loaf, etc., line the sides and bottom with parchment paper. Bake your product. If anything stuck to the pan, cool the pans to room temperature and soak them in cold water for 15 minutes. Wipe clean with a damp cloth. Do not scour. The next several times you use them, generously grease the sides and bottom.

26. Cleanup after kneading bread is simple if you do it immediately. After setting your kneaded dough to rise, scrape the counter surface with the bench scraper to pull up any residue.

27. Use a warm wet dishcloth to wipe the counter clear, scrubbing it as necessary to clean up any residue. Wipe the blade of the bench scraper clean before using it to form your loaves.

YEAST
BREADS

MULTIGRAIN BREAD:

Replace 1 cup whole wheat bread flour with ⅓ cup whole grain spelt flour, ⅓ cup whole grain cornmeal, and ⅓ cup rolled oats. Increase vital wheat gluten to ⅓ cup.

100% Whole Grain Bread

MAKES: a 9" loaf

PREP. TIME: 40 minutes

RISING TIME: approx. 1½ hours

BAKING TIME: 30–35 minutes

1¼ cups warm water *or* milk (110–115°F)

1 Tbsp. active dry yeast

¼ cup honey

3–3½ cups whole wheat bread flour, *divided*

¼ cup vital wheat gluten, *optional*

2–3 Tbsp. dry milk powder (omit if using milk)

2 Tbsp. oil *or* room temperature unsalted butter

½ tsp. vinegar

1¼ tsp. salt

¼ cup seeds and nuts of your choice, *optional*

bread flour, for kneading

Optional: Add ¼ cup ground flax seed to either variation.

1. Add all ingredients to large bowl in order listed, starting with just 3 cups of flour.
2. Stir and scrape the ingredients together. When it becomes too hard to stir, use your hand to bring the dough together.
3. Sprinkle some of the remaining ½ cup flour onto the work surface. Tip the bowl and scrape the dough onto the flour.
4. Using your hands or a bench scraper, work the dough into a soft ball. Knead it 1 minute.
5. Cover dough with a bowl, whose interior has been greased. Let rest 10 minutes to allow the gluten strands to come together.
6. Knead dough again for 8–10 minutes. Keep some of the ½ cup flour at the farthest side of your kneading surface to pick up a small dusting as needed each time you push the dough away from yourself. You may need more or less than ½ cup flour to get smooth, elastic dough.
7. Place dough upside down in the bowl. Then flip the greased side up.
8. Cover with damp linen kitchen towel. Set in warm, draft-free place to rise until double, approximately an hour. Dough is doubled when poked with 2 fingers and the indentation stays.
9. Gently punch down the dough. Tip the bowl as you release the dough from the sides of the bowl and let it roll onto non-floured work surface.
10. Pat or roll the dough into a rectangle approximately 8 × 12".
11. Start at a narrow end and roll dough up, jelly-roll style, into a loaf. Be careful not to trap air pockets as you roll it.
12. Place loaf seam-side down in well-greased 9×5" loaf pan. Cover with the towel. Allow to rise until almost double, approximately 30 minutes.
13. Bake in preheated 350°F oven for 30–35 minutes, until loaf sounds hollow when tapped sharply on the bottom.
14. Remove from pan and cool on wire rack.

Oatmeal Bread

If you prefer the oats to stay more intact, skip the soaking time.

MAKES: two 9" loaves

PREP. TIME: 30 minutes

RISING TIME: approx. 1½ hours

BAKING TIME: 30–40 minutes

1 cup rolled *or* quick oats

3 cups whole wheat bread flour, *divided*

¼ cup sugar *or* honey

1 Tbsp. active dry yeast

2½ cup warm water (110–115°F)

2 Tbsp. melted unsalted butter

⅓ cup dry milk powder

2½ tsp. salt

2 Tbsp. vital wheat gluten, *optional*

2–2½ cups bread flour

1. Place oats, 1 cup bread flour, sugar, and yeast in large bowl.
2. Pour the water over and stir. Let set 10 minutes to soak.
3. Stir in the remaining ingredients, reserving ½ cup bread flour.
4. Sprinkle work surface with some of the remaining flour. Tip and scrape the dough onto the work surface.
5. Using your hands or a bench scraper, work the dough into a ball. Knead 1 minute.
6. Cover dough with bowl, whose interior has been greased. Allow to rest 10 minutes to allow the gluten strands to come together.
7. Knead dough again for 8–10 minutes. Keep some of the ½ cup flour at the farthest side of your kneading surface to pick up a small dusting as needed each time you push the dough away from yourself. You may need more or less than ½ cup flour to get smooth, elastic dough.
8. Place dough upside down in the bowl. Then flip the greased side up.
9. Cover with damp linen kitchen towel. Set in warm, draft-free place to rise until double, approximately an hour. Dough is doubled when poked with 2 fingers and the indentation stays.
10. Gently punch down the dough. Tip the bowl as you release the dough from the sides of the bowl and let it roll onto non-floured work surface. Divide dough in half.
11. Pat or roll one half into a rectangle approximately 8×12".
12. Start at a narrow end and roll dough up, jelly-roll style, into a loaf. Be careful not to trap air pockets as you roll it.
13. Repeat with second half of dough.

14. If you wish, gently brush loaves with beaten egg and sprinkle with rolled oats.

15. Place loaves seam-side down in well-greased 9×5″ loaf pans. Cover with the towel. Allow to rise until almost double, approximately 30 minutes.

16. Bake in preheated 350°F oven for 30–40 minutes, until loaves sound hollow when tapped sharply on the bottom.

17. Remove from pan and cool on wire rack.

Oven baking times vary. My daughter and I have the extremes. Depending on what she's baking, hers can take up to 15 minutes longer than mine.

Spelt Bread

MAKES: two 9" loaves

PREP. TIME: 30 minutes

RISING TIME: approx. 1½ hours

BAKING TIME: 30–35 minutes

2⅓ cups warm water (110–115°F), *divided*

4 tsp. active dry yeast

½ tsp. sugar

3 Tbsp. honey

4 Tbsp. vital wheat gluten

½ tsp. vinegar

⅓ cup oil *or* unsalted butter, room temperature

2½ tsp. salt

4 cups whole grain spelt flour

2 cups whole wheat bread flour

½–1 cup all-purpose flour, *divided*

This bread makes delicious toast and is also good for sandwiches.

1. Combine ½ cup water, yeast, and sugar in mixing bowl. Set in a warm place until bubbly, about 5 minutes.

2. Add remaining ingredients, starting with ½ cup bread flour. Stir and scrape the ingredients together. When it becomes too hard to stir, use your hand to bring the dough together.

3. Sprinkle work surface with some of the remaining flour. Tip and scrape the dough onto the flour.

4. Using your hands or a bench scraper, work the dough into a ball. Knead it 1 minute.

5. Cover dough with bowl, whose interior has been greased. Let rest 10 minutes to allow the gluten strands to come together.

6. Knead dough again for 8–10 minutes. Keep some of the ½ cup flour at the farthest side of your kneading surface to pick up a small dusting as needed each time you push the dough away from yourself. You may need more or less than ½ cup flour to get smooth, elastic dough.

7. Place dough upside down in the bowl. Then flip the greased side up.

8. Cover with damp linen kitchen towel. Set in warm, draft-free place to rise until double, approximately an hour. Dough is doubled when poked with 2 fingers and the indentation stays.

9. Gently punch down the dough. Tip the bowl as you release the dough from the sides of the bowl and let it roll onto non-floured work surface. Divide dough in half.

10. Pat or roll one half into a rectangle approximately 8×12".

11. Start at a narrow end and roll dough up, jelly-roll style, into a loaf. Be careful not to trap air pockets as you roll it.

12. Repeat with second half of dough.

13. Place loaves seam-side down in well-greased 9×5″ loaf pans. Cover with the towel. Allow to rise until almost double, approximately 30 minutes.

14. Bake in preheated 350°F oven for 30–35 minutes, until loaves sound hollow when tapped sharply on the bottom.

15. Remove from pan and cool on wire rack.

Winter Squash Bread

MAKES: a 9" loaf or 12 rolls

PREP. TIME: 30 minutes

RISING TIME: approx. 1½ hours

BAKING TIME: 30–35 minutes

1 Tbsp. active dry yeast

2 Tbsp. warm water (110–115°F)

1 cup winter squash puree, warmed to 110–115°F

⅓ cup milk, warmed to 110–115°F

¼ cup (half stick) unsalted butter, melted

1 large egg, room temperature

3 Tbsp. brown sugar

1½ tsp. salt

1–3 Tbsp. vital wheat gluten, *optional*

2½ cups whole wheat bread flour

½–1 cup bread flour, *divided*

Makes delicious French toast (see page 233)! This makes lovely dinner rolls, too.

1. Add all ingredients to large bowl in order listed, starting with just ½ cup bread flour.

2. Stir and scrape the ingredients together. When it becomes too hard to stir, use your hand to bring the dough together.

3. Sprinkle some of the remaining bread flour onto the work surface. Tip the bowl and scrape the dough onto the flour.

4. Using your hands or a bench scraper, work the dough into a ball. Knead it 1 minute.

5. Cover dough with bowl, whose interior has been greased. Allow to rest 10 minutes to allow the gluten strands to come together.

6. Knead dough again for 8–10 minutes. Keep some of the ½ cup flour at the farthest side of your kneading surface to pick up a small dusting as needed each time you push the dough away from yourself. This keeps the dough from sticking as you are kneading. You may need more or less than ½ cup flour to get soft, smooth, elastic dough.

7. Place dough upside down in bowl. Then flip the greased side up.

8. Cover with damp linen kitchen towel. Set in warm, draft-free place to rise until double, approximately an hour. Dough is doubled when poked with 2 fingers and the indentation stays.

9. Gently punch down the dough. Tip the bowl as you release the dough from the sides of the bowl and let it roll onto non-floured work surface.

10. Pat or roll the dough into a rectangle approximately 8×12".

11. Start at a narrow end and roll dough up, jelly-roll style, into a loaf. Be careful not to trap air pockets as you roll it.

12. Place loaf seam-side down in well-greased 9×5" loaf pan. Cover with damp linen kitchen towel. Allow to rise until almost double, approximately 30 minutes.

13. Bake in preheated 350°F oven for 30–35 minutes, until loaf sounds hollow when tapped sharply on the bottom.

14. Remove from pan and cool on wire rack.

Whole Wheat Pizza Dough

MAKES: two 12" pizzas or six 6"–7" pizzas

PREP. TIME: 40 minutes

RISING TIME: 1½–3 hours

BAKING TIME: 4–8 minutes

1 cup + 2 Tbsp. warm water (110–115°F)

2¼ tsp. active dry yeast

1½ cups bread flour

1¾ cups whole wheat bread flour, *divided*

4 Tbsp. extra-virgin olive oil

1 tsp. salt

1–2 Tbsp. vital wheat gluten, *optional*

pizza toppings and sauce, whatever you like

Some pizza peels have a thick front edge, known to my family as a "bulldozer" edge. If yours tends to push the dough away rather than slide underneath, have someone slightly bevel the top front edge with a grinder.

1. Place warm water, yeast, and 1½ cups bread flour in large bowl. Whisk to combine.

2. Cover bowl with damp linen kitchen towel. Put in warm, draft-free place. Allow to set for at least 30 minutes and up to 3 hours. It will become quite foamy.

3. Stir down foamy mixture. Add olive oil, salt, and 1½ cups whole wheat bread flour.

4. Stir together with your hand. Add enough of the remaining flour to bring the dough together into a stiff but still workable dough.

5. Tip the dough onto the work surface. Knead several minutes. Grease the bowl.

6. Place dough upside down in bowl. Then flip the greased side up.

7. Cover with damp linen kitchen towel. Set in warm, draft-free place to rise until double, approximately an hour. Dough is doubled when poked with 2 fingers and the indentation stays.

8. When the dough has risen, gently turn it onto the non-floured work surface. Using a dough scraper, divide it into desired size pieces. Form each into a round using the dough scraper to tuck and roll it on the counter surface. Cover each with a damp towel or bowl and allow to rest at least 30 minutes or until the gluten relaxes enough to form your crusts. Test one as in step 10 of the instructions before heating your oven. If the dough wants to spring back it means it hasn't rested long enough. Don't fight it. Give it more rest time.

9. Center a flat pizza stone on a rack near the bottom of the oven. Preheat the oven to 475–500 degrees long enough to get the stone very hot, about 30–40 minutes. Or use an inverted half sheet which you put in the oven near the end of the preheat.

10. Sprinkle the work surface with whole wheat flour or whole cornmeal. Without deflating the dough, lift a ball onto the dusted area. Pressing with the ball of your fingertips, gently press and stretch the center of the dough into your desired thickness, keeping the outer edge untouched to form a puffy rim.

11. Use the bench scraper to lift the edges. Generously toss flour underneath to make it slide freely.

12. Place desired sauce and/or toppings on dough. Toppings MUST be cool or room temperature. Keep toppings away from the edge of the crust so they don't drop off and burn during baking.

13. Hold a pizza peel or flat, thin baking sheet level next to the pizza. Sprinkle its edge with flour. With a quick forward thrust, get the peel under the entire pizza, giving quick back-and-forth jerks as needed to get the pizza on entirely.

14. *Work quickly here!* Hold the peel level in the oven above the hot pizza stone an inch or two from back of the stone. With a quick backward jerk, pull the peel out so the pizza drops on the hot stone. Don't try to reposition the pizza. Close the oven door and bake for 5–8 minutes or until bubbly.

15. Set peel aside in cool place. An unbaked pizza will stick to a warmed peel.

16. To remove the hot pizza from the baking stone, thrust the peel all the way under the pizza. Place pizza on a wooden cutting board or thick kitchen towel. Cut and serve.

Start your dough early in the day to give it plenty of rest time after you have formed your balls of dough. It's better to let them rest longer than to fight active gluten. Everything will take longer in a chilly kitchen. In a rush, use the quick dough (page 191).

This is great dough for "thin crust" pizza lovers. It is not a yeast dough. It's more like a biscuit dough. It rolls super thin, yet is still workable.

Super Quick Pizza Dough

You can substitute regular yogurt in place of Greek yogurt. Start with a little less than a half cup, adding just a tablespoon or two more as needed to get a kneadable dough.

MAKES: a 12" – 14" pizza

PREP. TIME: 20 minutes

BAKING TIME: 5–8 minutes

½ cup whole wheat pastry flour

½ cup whole wheat bread flour *

½ cup all-purpose flour

2 tsp. baking powder

½ tsp. salt

½–1 cup not nonfat Greek yogurt, room temperature

* *You can use Multi Grain Mix (page 180) as part of your whole grain flour.*

1. In a large bowl, combine dry ingredients. Add ½ cup yogurt, adding the other ½ cup as needed to get a kneadable dough.

2. Knead several minutes until it is smooth and elastic. This is the rare biscuit dough that needs gluten action so it hangs together.

3. Roll on floured work surface to the thickness you want.

4. Follow forming and baking techniques as in Whole Wheat Pizza Dough, Steps 10–16, page 188–189.

Add in dried herbs for a flavorful crust.

Whole Wheat Pita Bread

MAKES: 8 pitas

PREP. TIME: 30 minutes

RISING TIME: approx. 1½ hours

BAKING TIME: 3 minutes per pita

> *I have used up to three-fourths whole wheat flour in the pitas with great results. Add vital wheat gluten accordingly. The dough needs it.*

1. Use the Whole Wheat Pizza Dough recipe on page 188 except use melted lard as some or all of the oil. Follow Steps 1–7

2. After the dough has risen, cut it into 8 equal pieces with a bench scraper.

3. On a lightly floured surface using a vertical rolling pin, roll each piece of dough into a 7" even-thickness round.

4. Allow rolled pitas to rest uncovered on a well-floured, draft-free surface for 30 minutes (longer if your surface is stone or otherwise cool). The pitas should look slightly puffy.

5. Place pizza stone on lowest racks of oven. Preheat oven to 500°F. The pizza stones need to be at 500°F for at least 10 minutes to be hot enough.

6. Hold a pizza peel or flat, thin baking sheet level next to a puffy pita. Sprinkle its edge with flour. With a quick forward thrust, get the peel under the entire pita, giving quick back-and-forth jerks as needed to get the pita on entirely.

7. Be careful not to bend the pita or handle it roughly because the rise might deflate and then the pitas won't puff up.

8. *Work quickly here!* Hold the peel level in the oven above the hot pizza stone an inch or two from back of the stone. Lay the pita on the hot stone with a quick backwards jerk. Don't try to reposition the pita. Place 1–2 pitas on each hot pizza stone.

9. Bake 2 minutes at 500°F. By this time they should have bubbled up and look like balloons. Flip them to the other side. Bake 1 minute longer. Remove to wire rack. Bake remaining pitas in the same manner.

10. When cool, the pitas may still be puffy. Seal in a large plastic bag for an hour so that they soften enough to flatten without cracking. Eat fresh, or halve and freeze.

Flour Tortillas

MAKES: eight 8" tortillas

PREP. TIME: 40 minutes

COOKING TIME: less than a minute for each tortilla

¾ cup whole wheat pastry flour

¾ cup whole wheat bread flour

½ cup all-purpose flour

1 tsp. salt

1 tsp. baking powder, optional

²/₃–¾ cup room temperature water

¹/₃ cup room temperature butter or high quality lard

To make multi-grain tortillas, replace whole wheat flours with ½ cup whole wheat pastry flour, ½ cup whole wheat bread flour, and ½ cup multigrain mix. Add 2 Tbsp. ground flax seed.

1. Mix dry ingredients in large bowl.

2. Add milk and oil. Mix and scrape sides of bowl.

3. Using your hands, knead into a ball.

4. Place ball on work surface and knead a few minutes to form a lovely, smooth, soft ball.

5. Use a bench scraper to divide dough into 8–10 equal size pieces.

6. Form each piece into a smooth ball by cupping your hand over it and using gentle pressure to roll until smooth. Flatten slightly and place each piece in a single layer in the bowl. Allow to rest for 30 minutes to relax the gluten.

7. Roll 1 disc into an 8" circle with a vertical rolling pin. Use the tiniest sprinkle of flour if you need to, but I prefer the dough to stick slightly to the work surface as I roll it. Flip it often as you roll it out.

8. Leave the rolled disc to rest to allow the gluten to relax while you roll out the next one.

9. Remove the first disc to a clean spot and cover with a dry linen kitchen towel. Stack remaining discs on top as they are rolled and rested, sprinkling the lightest bit of flour between them and keeping them covered with the dry towel.

10. Heat a large, ungreased cast-iron or heavy bottom skillet on high until very hot, almost smoking.

11. With both hands, pick up a tortilla and place it flat in

To serve later, allow the covered stack to cool on the counter top. Wrap the tortillas in the damp cloth and store in a zip-lock freezer bag with the air pressed out. Stored in this way, tortillas will keep for a week or more in the refrigerator.

the hot, ungreased skillet.

12. After 15–20 seconds, flip it. Cook another 15 seconds until lightly browned in spots. If a tortilla forms a bubble underneath, gently lift the edge and allow it to escape. Lower the heat if the tortillas are burning, but don't despair: the ones that have blackened spots taste like they are made over the open fire.

13. As they are cooked, encase the finished tortillas between a double layer of damp towels.

The most important tip when making and storing tortillas is keeping them wrapped in a clean, lightly dampened feedsack cloth or linen kitchen towel.

Hamburger or Hot Dog Buns

MAKES: 30 average size buns

PREP. TIME: 40 minutes

RISING TIME: approx. 1½ hours

BAKING TIME: 18–23 minutes

2½ cups warm water (110–115°F) *or* milk

2 Tbsp. active dry yeast

¼ cup sugar

3½ cups bread flour, *divided*

3 cups whole wheat bread flour

½ cup oil

1 large egg, room temperature, beaten, *divided* (reserve half to brush on tops of rolls before baking)

½ cup dry milk powder (omit if using milk)

2 tsp. salt

sesame seeds or poppy seeds for sprinkling on top

This recipe can easily be halved or doubled. The buns freeze well for up to 2 months if properly wrapped in freezer bags.

1. Add warm water, yeast, sugar, and 1 cup bread flour to large bowl. Whisk together.

2. Cover bowl with damp linen kitchen towel. Set in warm, draft-free place for 10–15 minutes until bubbly. Whisk well.

3. Add oil, half the beaten egg, milk powder, salt, 2 cups bread flour, and 3 cups whole wheat bread flour. Stir with a wooden spoon and then use your hands to get a soft workable dough.

4. Sprinkle a bit of the remaining ½ cup bread flour onto the work surface. Tip the bowl and scrape the dough onto the flour.

5. Knead 1 minute.

6. Cover dough with bowl, whose interior has been greased. Let rest 10 minutes to allow the gluten strands to come together.

7. Knead dough again for 4–5 minutes. Keep some of the ½ cup flour at the farthest side of your kneading surface to pick up a small dusting as needed to prevent sticking each time you push the dough away from yourself. You may need more or less than ½ cup flour to get a soft, elastic dough.

8. Return dough to the greased bowl. Flip the greased side up.

9. Cover with a damp towel. Set in warm, draft-free place to rise until double, approximately an hour. Dough is doubled when poked with 2 fingers and the indentation stays.

10. Gently punch down the dough. Tip the bowl as you release the dough from the sides of the bowl and let it roll onto non-floured work surface.

11. Gently shape dough into flat oval. Cut in half with bench scraper, setting one half aside.

12. Score and cut each half into 15 even pieces. Scrape up a piece. Form it into a flat round disc about 3–3½" across and ¾" thick. The center should be a bit thinner than the outer edges. Repeat with other pieces.

13. Place discs about 1" apart on parchment-lined baking sheets.

14. Cover dough discs with the towel. Allow to rise until nearly double, approximately 20–30 minutes.

15. Preheat oven to 350°F while rolls are rising. Very gently brush tops of each roll with remaining beaten egg. Sprinkle with seeds if desired.

16. Bake in preheated 350°F oven for 13 minutes, then switch the pans and bake 5–7 minutes longer until rolls are golden and springy when lightly touched. Do not overbake.

17. Slide parchment containing rolls onto wire racks. Cool completely before slicing, serving, or freezing.

To make Hot Dog Buns, shape dough into long narrow shapes, about 1 × 5".

Cracked Wheat Rolls

MAKES: 18 dinner rolls

PREP. TIME: 40 minutes

SOAKING TIME: 45 minutes

RISING TIME: approx. 1½ hours

BAKING TIME: 18–25 minutes

½ cup cracked wheat

3 tsp. salt, *divided*

1½ cups boiling water

1 Tbsp. honey

1 Tbsp. active dry yeast

1½ cup warm milk
(110–115°F)

7 Tbsp. unsalted butter *or* oil

¼ cup warm water
(110–115°F)

1½ cups whole wheat bread
flour

2½–3 cups all-purpose flour,
divided

1 egg white, room
temperature, lightly
beaten

Sesame, poppy, *or* flax seeds
optional

1. Place cracked wheat and ½ tsp. salt in a small heatproof bowl. Pour boiling water over and allow to soak at least 45 minutes.

2. When cracked wheat is still warm, drain and place in a large bowl.

3. Add honey, yeast, milk, butter, remaining 2½ tsp. salt, water, whole wheat bread flour, and 2½ cups all-purpose flour. Stir with a wooden spoon and then your hands to get the softest dough you can possibly work with.

4. Sprinkle some of the remaining ½ cup bread flour onto the work surface. Tip the bowl and scrape the dough onto the flour.

5. Work the dough into a ball. Knead it 1 minute.

6. Cover dough with bowl, whose interior has been greased. Let rest 10 minutes to allow the gluten strands to come together.

7. Knead for 3–4 minutes. Keep some of the ½ cup flour at the farthest side of your kneading surface to pick up a small dusting as needed to prevent sticking each time you push the dough away from yourself. You may need more or less than ½ cup flour to get smooth, elastic dough. Keep in mind that the softer the dough, the more tender the rolls.

8. Return dough to the bowl. Flip to have the greased side up.

9. Cover with a lightly dampened towel. Set in warm, draft-free place to rise until double, approximately an hour. Dough is doubled when poked with 2 fingers and the indentation stays.

10. Gently punch down the dough. Tip the bowl as you release the dough from the sides of the bowl and let it roll onto non-floured work surface.

11. Roll and ease the dough into a 2" rope. Cut rope into 18 equal pieces with bench scraper.

12. On a non-floured work surface (to give a little resistance), cup hand around a piece of dough. Curl your fingers around the ball. Working in small circles, roll into a ball with moderate pressure from your fingers and the heel of your hand, feeling the resistance as you roll it. The resulting roll should be smooth and round and have a dimple in the bottom. Repeat with remaining pieces.

13. Arrange ½–1" apart on parchment-lined rimmed baking sheet. The amount of space between rolls determines how much they spread during rising and baking. For tall "break apart" rolls, place balls against each other in the pan.

14. Cover with the towel. Allow to rise until almost double, approximately 30 minutes.

15. Brush gently with egg white. Sprinkle with seeds if desired.

16. Bake in preheated 350°F oven for 18–25 minutes until golden and hollow-sounding when rapped on the bottom of the pan.

17. Slide parchment with rolls onto cooling rack.

These rolls are light and melt-in-your-mouth delicious.

Rosemary Garlic Bread

MAKES: a 14" loaf

PREP. TIME: 30 minutes

RISING TIME: approx. 1½ hours

BAKING TIME: 53–58 minutes

1 large head (bulb) of garlic

2 tsp. extra-virgin olive oil

1–2 Tbsp. minced fresh rosemary *or* 1–2 tsp. dried

⅓ cup unsalted chicken broth (110–115°F), *divided*

1 Tbsp. active dry yeast

1 tsp. sugar

½ cup warm milk (110–115°F)

2 Tbsp. unsalted butter, melted

1½ cups bread flour, *divided*

1 large egg, beaten, 1 Tbsp. reserved for brushing top of loaf

1 tsp. salt

1½ cups whole wheat bread flour

garlic salt, for sprinkling

You can bake the garlic bulb a day or two ahead along with something else you are baking in the oven. Store it covered with extra-virgin olive oil. Drain before using, saving the flavored oil to replace the butter in this recipe or for another recipe.

1. Remove papery outer skin from garlic bulb, leaving root end intact. Slice across upper tips. Place cut side up in a small baking dish. Drizzle with olive oil and sprinkle with rosemary. Cover and bake at 425°F for 30–40 minutes until softened. Cool 10 minutes.

2. Squeeze each softened clove into a bowl, discarding papery skins.

3. Add 2 tsp. of broth. Mash together lightly. Set aside.

4. Stir together yeast, sugar, remaining broth, milk, butter, and 1¼ cups bread flour in large bowl. Set in a warm place until bubbly, about 5 minutes.

5. Add egg, mashed garlic, salt, and 1½ cups whole wheat bread flour. Stir and scrape together to make a soft workable dough.

6. Sprinkle work surface with some of the remaining ¼ cup bread flour. Tip the bowl and scrape the dough onto the flour.

7. Knead dough for 5–7 minutes. To prevent sticking, keep some of the remaining flour at the farthest side of your kneading surface to pick up a small dusting as needed each time you push the dough away from yourself. You may need more or less than ¼ cup flour to get smooth, elastic dough.

8. Grease interior of bowl. Return dough to bowl. Flip to have greased side up.

9. Cover with lightly dampened towel. Set in warm, draft-free place to rise until double, approximately an hour. Dough is doubled when poked with 2 fingers and the indentation stays.

10. Gently punch down the dough. Tip the bowl as you release the dough from the sides of the bowl and let it roll onto non-floured work surface.

11. Pat or roll the dough into an 8×12" rectangle.

12. Start at a wide end and use bench scraper to release dough from work surface. Roll dough up, jelly-roll style. Be careful not to trap air pockets as you roll it. Pinch and seal seam along entire length of roll. Stretch and coax the roll into a 14" loaf, tucking ends as needed and pinching to keep in place.

13. Place loaf seam-side down on parchment lined baking sheet. Cover with the towel.

14. Allow to rise in warm, draft-free place until nearly doubled, approximately 30 minutes.

15. Gently brush with reserved 1 Tbsp. beaten egg. Sprinkle with garlic salt.

16. Bake in preheated 350°F oven for 23–28 minutes, until golden and hollow-sounding when tapped on the bottom.

For a richer loaf, add 1 Tbsp. extra butter to the dough and skip the egg wash. Instead, bake 15 minutes. Melt 1 Tbsp. butter and stir in ½ tsp. garlic salt. Brush this on the partially baked loaf. Bake 10–15 minutes longer until done.

You can cut the risen dough into 2 or 3 strips. For 2 strips, twist and tuck ends as in photo. For 3 strips, braid as in Egg Braid, pages 204–205.

Parmesan Cheese Bread

MAKES: a 14" loaf, or 9 dinner rolls

PREP. TIME: 40 minutes

RISING TIME: approx. 1½ hours

BAKING TIME: 25–35 minutes

1 cup warm water (110–115°F)

1 Tbsp. active dry yeast

2 tsp. sugar

1½ cups whole wheat bread flour

¾–1 cup bread flour, *divided*

1 Tbsp. vital wheat gluten, *optional*

¼ cup oil, may use all or part extra-virgin olive oil, *or* melted and cooled unsalted butter

1 large egg, lightly beaten, 2 tsp. reserved for brushing loaf

1–2 Tbsp. finely minced *or* grated onion, *or* 1 tsp. onion powder

½–1 tsp. granulated garlic

1 tsp. salt

½–⅔ cup fresh, finely grated Parmesan cheese

crushed dried Italian herbs *or* coarse salt, for sprinkling

1. Lightly whisk the water, yeast, and sugar in a large, warm bowl. Allow to foam a bit.

2. Add remaining ingredients in order given, using ¾ cup bread flour. Stir and work the dough into a soft ball.

3. Sprinkle work surface with some of the remaining ¼ cup bread flour. Tip the bowl and scrape the dough onto the flour.

4. Knead for 1 minute.

5. Cover dough with bowl, whose interior has been greased. Allow to rest 10 minutes to allow the gluten strands to come together.

6. Knead dough again for 4–6 minutes. Keep the remaining ¼ cup flour at the farthest side of your kneading surface to pick up a small dusting as needed each time you push the dough away from yourself. You may need more or less than ¼ cup flour to get smooth, elastic dough.

7. Return dough to the greased bowl. Flip to expose the greased side.

8. Cover with damp linen kitchen towel. Set in warm, draft-free place to rise until double, approximately an hour. Dough is doubled when poked with 2 fingers and the indentation stays.

9. Gently punch down the dough. Tip the bowl as you release the dough from the sides of the bowl and let it roll onto non-floured work surface.

10. Pat or roll the dough into an 8×12" rectangle.

11. Start at a wide end and use bench scraper to release dough from work surface. Roll dough up, jelly-roll style. Be careful not to trap air pockets as you roll it. Pinch and seal seam along entire length of roll. Stretch and coax the roll into a 14" loaf, tucking ends as needed and pinching to keep in place.

12. Place loaf seam-side down on parchment-lined baking sheet. Cover with the towel.

13. Allow to rise in warm, draft-free place until nearly doubled, approximately 30 minutes.

14. Gently brush with reserved 2 tsp. beaten egg. Sprinkle with Italian herbs or coarse salt.

15. Bake in preheated 350°F oven for 25–35 minutes, until golden and hollow-sounding when tapped on the bottom.

16. Slide parchment with loaf onto wire rack to cool.

loaf of this bread makes a lovely display as communion bread.

Egg Braid

MAKES: two 14", tender, delightfully golden braids

PREP. TIME: 40 minutes

RISING TIME: approx. 1½ hours

BAKING TIME: 20–30 minutes

½ cup warm water (110–115°F)

1 Tbsp. active dry yeast

1½ cups warm milk (110–115°F)

2 Tbsp. sugar

2 tsp. salt

3 Tbsp. unsalted butter at room temperature, *or oil*

3 large eggs, room temperature, 1 egg separated and white reserved

2 cups whole wheat bread flour

4½ cups bread flour, *divided*

You can halve this recipe using 2 small or 1½ large eggs. Reserve a tiny bit of one egg white for brushing.

1. Place water and yeast in a large warm bowl.

2. When bubbly, add remaining ingredients, reserving 1 egg white and ½ cup bread flour. Stir and scrape the ingredients together into a workable dough.

3. Sprinkle work surface with some of the remaining ½ cup bread flour. Tip the bowl and scrape the dough onto the flour.

4. Using your hands or the bench scraper, work the dough into a ball. Knead it 1 minute.

5. Cover dough with bowl, whose interior has been greased. Let rest 10 minutes to allow the gluten strands to come together.

6. Knead dough again for 4–5 minutes. Keep some of the ½ cup flour at the farthest side of your kneading surface to pick up a small dusting as needed each time you push the dough away from you. This keeps the dough from sticking as you are kneading. You may need more or less than ½ cup flour to get smooth, elastic dough.

7. Return dough to the greased bowl. Flip the greased side up.

8. Cover with damp linen kitchen towel. Set in warm, draft-free place to rise until double, approximately an hour. Dough is doubled when poked with 2 fingers and the indentation stays.

9. Gently punch down the dough. Tip the bowl as you release the dough from the sides of the bowl and let it roll onto non-floured work surface.

10. Divide dough in half.

11. Divide one half of the dough into 3 equal parts. If it sticks, use the bench scraper to free it from the surface.

12. Roll each thin piece into an 18" rope. Pinch the three ropes together at one end. Braid. Pinch ends together and tuck under.

13. Place on parchment-lined baking sheet. Repeat cutting, braiding, pinching with other half of dough.

14. Cover braids with towel. Allow braids to rise until nearly double, approximately 30 minutes.

15. Beat reserved egg white slightly. Brush gently on loaves, hitting the high spots of the braid.

16. Bake in preheated 350°F oven for 20–30 minutes until golden and sounds hollow when tapped on the bottom. You may want to switch the racks after 12 minutes baking time.

17. Slide parchment papers containing the loaves onto wire racks. Cool.

Any leftovers after a day or two can be used to make delicious French toast (see page 232–233).

Baked Apple Fritters

MAKES: 12 fritters

PREP. TIME: 30 minutes

RISING TIME: approx. 1½ hours

BAKING TIME: 20–25 minutes

FILLING:

2½ cups finely diced, peeled, tart apples

1½ tsp. fresh lemon juice if your apples are not tart, *optional*

2–4 Tbsp. sugar, depending on the sweetness of your apples

½ tsp. ground cinnamon

1 Tbsp. Clear Jel (not instant) *or* cornstarch

1 Tbsp. water

DOUGH:

½ cup milk, warmed to 110–115°F

½ cup all-purpose flour

1¼ cups whole wheat bread flour, *divided*

½ tsp. + ¼ cup sugar, divided

1½ tsp. active dry yeast

2 Tbsp. unsalted butter, softened

½ tsp. salt

1 small egg, room temperature

GLAZE:

¾ cup confectioners sugar

2 tsp. unsalted butter, softened

dash salt

2–4 tsp. milk *or* apple cider

¼ tsp. vanilla extract

1. Stir filling ingredients together in a heavy kettle. Cook and stir until thickened and apples are just soft. Set aside to cool completely.

2. Stir together milk, bread flour, ½ tsp. sugar, and yeast in large bowl.

3. Cover with a damp linen kitchen towel. Set in a warm place until bubbly, about 20 minutes.

4. Stir down. Add 1 cup whole wheat bread flour, ¼ cup sugar, butter, salt, and egg. Stir into a very soft dough.

5. Sprinkle work surface with some of the remaining ¼ cup bread flour. Tip the bowl and scrape the dough onto the flour. Using your hands and a bench scraper, work the dough into a ball.

6. Knead dough several minutes. Keep some of the ¼ cup flour at the farthest side of your kneading surface to pick up a small dusting as needed to keep dough from sticking each time you push the dough away from yourself. This should be very tender dough.

7. Grease the bowl and return dough to the bowl. Flip the greased side up.

8. Cover with very lightly dampened towel. Set in warm, draft-free place to rise until double, approximately an hour. Dough is doubled when poked with 2 fingers and the indentation stays.

9. Gently punch down the dough. Tip the bowl as you release the dough from the sides of the bowl and let it roll onto non-floured work surface.

10. Roll into 12×16" rectangle. It's okay if it sticks to the counter.

11. Let stand a few minutes to relax. Using a pizza cutter or bench scraper, cut into 12 4" squares (2 lengthwise cuts, 3 crosswise cuts).

12. Place about 1½ Tbsp. cooled filling in the center of each square. Using bench scraper, lift the 4 corners of 1 square and pinch together at the top.

13. Pick up with floured scraper and place in well-greased 9×13" baking pan. Repeat for remaining squares, spacing evenly in pan.

14. Cover pan of fritters with the towel. Allow to rise until nearly double, approximately 30 minutes.

15. Bake in preheated 350°F oven for 20–25 minutes. The fritters will bake together. Lift up a corner of a center fritter to make certain it isn't doughy.

16. Allow fritters to cool until barely warm so the glaze can just slightly soak into the fritters.

17. To make the glaze, combine glaze ingredients in a bowl, starting with only 2 tsp. milk. Whisk, adding tiny amounts of liquid at a time, until glaze is thick but pourable. Drizzle glaze over fritters.

A super tender dough is hard to handle, so do the best you can. The fritters may not look perfect, but they bake up fine and are delicious.

Fruited Breakfast Rolls

MAKES: 12 large rolls

PREP. TIME: 30 minutes

RISING TIME: approx. 1½ hours

BAKING TIME: 25–30 minutes

1 Tbsp. active dry yeast

1 Tbsp. sugar

2½ cups warm (not skim) milk (110–115°F)

2 tsp. salt

2–3 Tbsp. vital wheat gluten, *optional*

3 cups whole wheat bread flour

2½ cups all-purpose flour, *divided*

14½ oz. jar apricot spreadable fruit *or* jam of your choice

ground cinnamon, *optional*

GLAZE:

1 cup confectioners sugar

2 tsp. unsalted butter, softened

2–4 tsp. milk *or* remaining fruit spread

tiny pinch salt

¼ tsp. vanilla extract

1–2 drops almond extract, *optional*

sliced almonds for garnishing, *optional*

1. Stir together yeast, sugar, and milk in large bowl. Set in a warm place until bubbly, about 5 minutes.

2. Add salt, optional gluten, whole wheat bread flour, and 2 cups all-purpose flour. Stir and work with hands to make a tender, workable dough.

3. Sprinkle work surface with flour. Tip the bowl and release the dough onto prepared work surface. Knead 1 minute.

4. Cover dough with bowl, whose interior has been greased. Let rest 10 minutes to allow the gluten strands to come together.

5. Knead dough again for several minutes. Keep some of the ½ cup flour at the farthest side of your kneading surface to pick up a small dusting as needed each time you push the dough away from yourself. This should be a soft dough.

6. Return dough to the bowl, whose interior has been greased. Flip the greased side up.

7. Cover with lightly dampened towel. Set in warm, draft-free place to rise until double, approximately an hour. Dough is doubled when poked with 2 fingers and the indentation stays.

8. Gently punch down the dough. Tip the bowl as you release the dough from the sides of the bowl and let it roll onto non-floured work surface. It's okay if it sticks.

9. Using a vertical rolling pin, gently form the dough into an 18×18" rectangle.

> *Make the size rolls you desire by rolling the dough into different size rectangles in Step 9.*

10. Spread 1 cup of the fruit spread to within 1" of the top and bottom edge. Sprinkle with cinnamon if you wish.

11. Using your bench scraper to lift the dough, loosely roll it up, jelly-roll style. Pinch seam to seal.

12. Cut roll into 12 equal pieces. Lay them on their cut sides in a greased 9×13" baking pan.

13. Cover with the towel. Allow to rise until almost double, approximately 30 minutes.

14. Bake in preheated 350°F oven for 25–30 minutes, checking a roll in the middle of the pan for doneness.

15. Cool on a wire rack until barely warm.

16. Whisk together glaze ingredients, using just enough liquid to make a pourable glaze.

17. Drizzle rolls with glaze.

Potato Dough Baked Goods

MAKES: About 3 dozen rolls, depending upon which kind you choose to make

1 large potato, 8 oz. peeled weight

2 cups warm milk, (110–115°F)

½ cup (1 stick) unsalted butter, softened

½ cup + 1 tsp. sugar, *divided*

4–5 cups bread flour, *divided*

1 egg, room temperature

½ cup warm water (110–115°F)

1½ Tbsp. active dry yeast

1 Tbsp. salt

2 cups whole wheat pastry flour

1 Tbsp. vital wheat gluten, *optional*

Never use leftover mashed potatoes to make this dough. They have too many add-ins. Additionally, the chemical makeup of cooked potatoes changes very quickly, inhibiting the yeast and gluten action.

If you must, use ⅔ cup potato flakes and add enough hot water to make 1 cup mashed potatoes.

---

1. Peel potato. Dice into ½" cubes. Cover and cook in a small amount of water until fork tender. Drain and mash with back of fork.

2. Blend warm milk and very hot potato together until smooth with an immersion blender or in a stand blender.

3. Pour mixture into large bowl. Thoroughly scrape out container.

4. Whisk in butter, sugar, beaten egg and 1½ cups bread flour. Let cool to 110–115°F.

5. In a small bowl, whisk the ½ cup warm water, ½ tsp. sugar, and yeast. Let set to foam up.

6. Thoroughly whisk yeast mixture into potato mixture. Cover and set in a warm place to form a sponge, 30–40 minutes.

7. When it's quite foamy and bubbly, beat it and mix it well.

8. Stir in salt, whole wheat pastry flour, and 2½–3½ cups all-purpose bread flour. This dough is at its best when worked as sticky as is manageable. If you are a beginner, add the greater amount of flour.

9. Gently release dough from sides of bowl. Tip bowl on its side so dough rolls out onto floured work surface. Knead a few minutes if you can, or use a bench scraper to lift and fold the dough until it becomes elastic. It's fine if the dough is a bit shaggy.

10. Return dough to greased bowl. Flip greased side of dough up. Cover with lightly dampened towel. Set in warm, draft-free place and allow to rise until at least

double, approximately an hour. Dough is doubled when you poke it with 2 fingers and the indentation stays.

11. Gently punch down risen dough. Release dough from sides of bowl. As the dough is spilling out use a bench scraper to cut against the edge of the bowl to get a chunk onto the floured work surface. Set the bowl with the remaining dough aside.

12. Use a light, quick touch. The less you work the dough, the more tender the finished product. It's okay if it sticks to the counter surface. Your bench scraper will lift it off. Form the dough into dinner rolls, cinnamon rolls, a Swedish tea ring, sticky buns, pull-apart bread, or doughnuts. Instructions follow.

Recipes Using Potato Dough

Dinner Rolls
Page 212

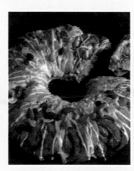

Swedish Tea Ring
Page 213

Cinnamon Rolls
Page 214

Pull-Apart Bread
Page 216

Doughnuts
Page 218

Dinner Rolls

Form and bake rolls using the method on page 198–199.

Swedish Tea Ring

1. Line a large rimmed baking pan with parchment paper.

2. Use at least ⅓ of the dough. Roll it into a ¼–⅜" thick rectangle.

3. Spread with 2 Tbsp. soft butter except for a 1" strip on one long side.

4. Sprinkle with a mixture of ½ cup sugar and 2–3 tsp. cinnamon, avoiding the ½" strip.

5. Starting on the opposite side, using your bench scraper to lift as you go, roll up jelly-roll style. Stop rolling 2" from the end. Use your bench scraper to lift the non-sugared edge up onto the roll. Pinch and seal. If your dough is impossibly sticky, sprinkle the work surface with flour the full length of the roll. Roll it seam-side down onto the flour.

6. Bring the 2 ends of the roll together to form a ring. Pinch together.

7. Place the ring on the prepared pan with the seam down.

8. Using a kitchen shears, lift and cut ⅔ of the way through the ring at 1" intervals. Be careful not to snip the paper. Fan the slices out to expose the cut edge.

9. Cover with a towel. Allow to rise until nearly double.

10. Bake in preheated 350°F oven for 20–30 minutes until golden and fully baked in the center. Slide parchment and Ring onto wire rack to cool.

11. When slightly warm, glaze with half a recipe of Glaze (see Step 9 of Cinnamon Rolls on page 214). Before the glaze forms a crust, sprinkle with nuts, chopped dried fruit, or colored sugar.

Cinnamon Rolls

1. Using ¼–⅓ of the dough, roll it into a 9" square ¼–⅜" thick.

2. Spread with 1½ Tbsp. softened butter except for a ½" strip on the edge that's toward you. For a lower fat version, spray with water until slightly glassy.

3. Sprinkle with a mixture of ¼ cup sugar and 2 tsp. cinnamon, avoiding the ½" strip.

4. Starting on the opposite side, using your bench scraper to lift as you go, roll up jelly-roll style. Don't roll too tightly or the center of the rolls will pop out while baking. Stop rolling 2" from the end. Use your bench scraper to lift the non-sugared edge up onto the roll. Pinch and seal. If your dough is impossibly sticky, sprinkle the work surface with flour the full length of the roll. Roll it seam-side down onto the flour.

5. Cut into 1"-thick slices. Place cut side up in a well-greased 8 or 9" pan.

6. Cover with a towel and let rise until nearly double. To make the rolls extra moist, just before baking, pour warmed cream, half-and-half, or whole milk over the rolls until almost level with the tops of the rolls. If your pan is deep enough, go to the tops of the rolls.

7. Bake in preheated 350°F oven for 20–25 minutes or until no longer doughy in the center. Cool.

8. Glaze while slightly warm. The glaze should barely melt in.

9. Glaze: whisk together 1 cup confectioners sugar, a tiny pinch salt, ¼ tsp. vanilla extract, and enough room temperature water to make a glaze that drizzles but mostly stays on top of the rolls.

TO MAKE STICKY BUNS:

1. Make goo by stirring together ¼ cup brown sugar, 1 Tbsp. white corn syrup, 1 Tbsp. softened unsalted butter, and 1 Tbsp. water.

2. Grease the bottom and sides of a 9" metal baking pan (pottery, glass, and ceramic pans cause the sticky bun goo to caramelize and get hard). Spread goo in the bottom. Sprinkle with chopped nuts if desired.

3. Prepare the dough the same as for Cinnamon Rolls steps # 1–6, but placing the cut slices on top of the goo in the metal pan.

4. After they are baked, invert immediately onto a platter or cookie sheet.

We devour this as is, but you may glaze it with a half batch of the Cinnamon Roll Glaze (see Step 9 on page 214).

Pull-Apart Bread

1. Using ⅓ of the dough, roll dough into a rectangle, approximately 10×12".
2. Spread with 2 Tbsp. soft unsalted butter. Sprinkle with ⅓ cup sugar and 2 tsp. cinnamon.
3. Using a bench scraper, cut the short length into 5 or 6 strips, 10" long.
4. Stack the strips. Don't worry if the strips are uneven.
5. Cut stack into 4 even pieces.
6. Place the 4 layered pieces into a well-buttered 9×4" loaf pan like slices of bread. It's okay if they don't perfectly line up. Spread them out a bit so that they aren't all at one end.
7. Cover with a towel and set aside to rise until double.
8. Bake in preheated 350°F oven for 30–35 minutes, until golden brown on top and hollow-sounding when the bottom is tapped. Cool for 2 minutes in the pan. Lay the pan on its side on the cooling rack and slide the loaf out. Be careful not to mash it—it's incredibly tender. Set it up to cool completely.

Make several pull-apart loaves. Wrap them well and freeze them to have on hand to serve to unexpected overnight guests. You'll be their friend for life.

If I even hint that I'm possibly considering thinking about making doughnuts, my children from as far away as New York will be at my doorstep.

Doughnuts

To make baked doughnuts: place formed doughnuts 2" apart on greased baking sheet. Set to rise until nearly double. Bake at 350°F until baked through, about 10–15 minutes. While hot, brush with melted butter and dip in cinnamon sugar.

TOOLS NEEDED: *

- Deep fryer. "Fry Baby" is great for small amounts, or you can use an electric skillet.
- A doughnut cutter is a plus.
- ½" dowel sticks for hanging the glazed doughnuts.
- Wire frying ladle (reduces the amount of fat that's dragged from the fryer to the newspaper).

* *You can improvise on all these tools. It's just that these work well for me.*

You can use all of the dough and make 3 dozen average to large doughnuts or reduce the amounts of ingredients and make just a few doughnuts.

1. Prepare the dough as instructed on page 210–211. The stickier the dough, the more tender the doughnuts.
2. After the dough has risen, gently punch it down and turn half of it onto a lightly floured surface.
3. Pat ¾" thick.
4. Starting at the very edge, cut the doughnuts with a donut cutter. Cut them out right up against each other. You want to get as many out of your dough as possible before re-patting, because each time you work the dough, it gets a little tougher. Place doughnuts 2" apart on a parchment-lined and floured cookie sheet. Continue until you have as many as desired.
5. Cover the doughnuts with a dry towel and allow to double in size, about 45 minutes.
6. Heat oil to 375°F, enough oil to allow doughnuts to float freely, about 2" deep. Lard is best. Don't use olive oil.
7. In a large bowl, whisk together your glaze. (See Step 9 under Cinnamon Rolls on page 214, but add a little more water for a thinner glaze.) The number of doughnuts determines the amount of glaze.
8. After the dough has doubled in size, scrape up a donut as gently as possible and place it (don't drop it) in the hot fat. It will bubble and hiss and spit and float all around. When bubbling in the center of the doughnut is decreasing, flip it

over and fry it until the bubbling has nearly stopped. Experiment with this. You will soon know how much time it takes for each side.

9. Use a wire frying ladle to remove each doughnut to a pan lined with about 10 layers of newspaper.

10. Allow each doughnut to cool a minute, then dip it into the glaze if you wish, flipping it to coat completely. Hang it on a dowel stick placed over the glaze bowl (that's why you needed the large bowl for the glaze). When the glaze is finished dripping, the doughnut can be placed on a parchment-lined baking sheet to cool completely. It can be a 2 person job if you make the whole batch.

11. Resist the temptation to eat the doughnuts immediately. They are at their best 1–3 hours later. The next morning they are still good, but the glaze will have melted into the doughnut and the crustiness will be gone.

12. After you are done frying the last doughnut, clarify the fat by frying a few slices of potato in it. Remove the potato pieces, and turn off the heat. Cool the fat. Store in airtight container or tightly lidded jar and freeze to use for 1–2 more frying sessions.

13. Freeze leftover glaze to glaze cinnamon rolls or your next doughnuts.

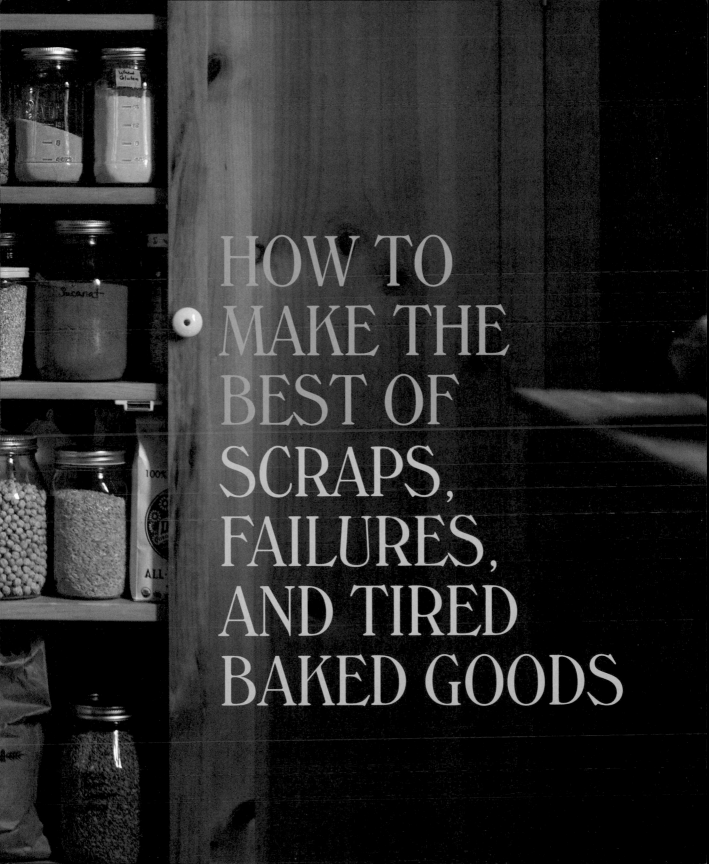

HOW TO MAKE THE BEST OF SCRAPS, FAILURES, AND TIRED BAKED GOODS

I prefer to use mostly chicken broth for a lighter flavor.

Filling Balls

MAKES: 9 balls

PREP. TIME: 20 minutes

BAKING TIME: 20–25 minutes

4 cups whole grain bread cubes, ½" dice

2–3 Tbsp. finely minced onion

⅓ cup finely minced celery

1 Tbsp. chopped fresh parsley *or* 1 tsp. dried

¼–½ tsp. salt

¼ tsp. pepper

½–¾ cup milk *or* chicken broth *or* combination, room temperature

1 large egg, beaten

½ cup mashed potatoes *

3 Tbsp. melted butter

* *I prefer to use fresh mashed potatoes, but you can use leftovers and adjust the seasonings to taste.*

1. Place the cubed bread, onion, celery, parsley, salt and pepper in a large bowl.
2. Whisk together the milk or broth, eggs and mashed potatoes.
3. Pour egg mixture over the bread.
4. Drizzle with melted butter. Mix lightly until just combined.
5. Divide mixture into 9 parts and shape into balls.
6. Place balls of filling in 9×9" greased baking pan.
7. Bake uncovered in preheated 350°F oven for 20–25 minutes or until golden and no longer gooey in the center.

If your bread is heavy, dice it finer. Or make it into coarse crumbs and use just 3 cups. The lighter the structure of the bread, the fluffier the filling balls. If you remove the outer crusts, it makes the balls fancier.

Add a little more liquid if you like super-moist filling to spread in a pan. Spread the mixture in a greased 8 × 8 pan instead of forming into balls.

Serve alongside your Thanksgiving turkey or use leftover turkey and broth to make turkey gravy to serve over the filling balls.

Add cubed turkey or chicken to the mixture and make Amish Roasht. Or use the lesser amount of liquid and form into patties. Fry in butter. Put in greased baking dish and bake a bit longer. Serve with gravy.

For added flavor, drizzle the balls with additional melted butter before baking.

Breakfast Casserole

MAKES: 9 × 13" casserole

PREP. TIME: 20 minutes

CHILLING TIME: several hours or overnight

STANDING TIME: 30 minutes, then 10 minutes

BAKING TIME: 45–60 minutes

6 ½"-thick slices whole grain bread, diced, *or* equivalent amount to cover the bottom of the baking pan

2 cups shredded cheese; preferably a combination of aged cheeses

4–6 slices bacon, fried and crumbled

½ cup diced green *or* red bell pepper, fresh, roasted, *or* frozen

10 large eggs

2½ cups milk

1 tsp. salt

½ tsp. dry mustard powder

¼ tsp. black pepper

¼ tsp. garlic powder *or* granules

¼ tsp. dried oregano

¼ tsp. paprika

ketchup *or* salsa, for serving, *optional*

1. Place diced bread in well-buttered 9×13" baking pan. The bread should cover the bottom.
2. Sprinkle evenly with cheese, bacon, and diced pepper.
3. In a large bowl whisk the eggs. Add and whisk in the milk and seasonings.
4. Pour egg mixture over the layers in the casserole dish.
5. Cover. Refrigerate several hours or overnight.
6. Let stand at room temperature for 30 minutes before baking.
7. Bake uncovered in preheated 350°F oven for 45–60 minutes until the middle is set (shaky but not liquid-y) and the edges are golden brown. Don't overbake. It will set up as it cools.
8. Let stand 10 minutes before serving. Serve with ketchup or salsa as a topping, if you wish.

This casserole is a great way to use up stale, too dry, or overbaked bread. Save the end crust for bread crumbs. Too much crust toughens the casserole.

Add other lightly sautéed, chopped vegetables or sliced black olives.

You may use another browned meat of your choice. 1–2 cups sausage, ham or a combination of meats. Add more or less meat to your liking. Omit it altogether for vegetarians.

Bake, cover with foil, wrap in a blanket, and take along to a carry-in breakfast or brunch.

If you have a failed or stale batch of cookies, make them into crumbs for these muffins, but omit the sugar and decrease the butter in the muffins by approximately 1 Tbsp. each.

If you want a dessert muffin, then don't decrease the sugar and fat.

old in chopped herbs, chopped nuts, pumpkin or sunflower seeds, flax seed, etc. The sky's the limit!

The Sky's the Limit Crumb Muffins

MAKES: 12 muffins

PREP. TIME: 20 minutes

BAKING TIME: 12–18 minutes

1 large egg, room temperature

1 cup less 2 Tbsp. milk, room temperature

¼ cup (half stick) unsalted butter, melted

1 cup dry bread crumbs

½ cup whole wheat pastry flour

½ cup whole wheat bread flour

1 Tbsp. sugar

¼ tsp. salt

1 Tbsp. baking powder

½ cup grated hard cheese, such as sharp cheddar *or* Parmesan

1. In a bowl, lightly beat the egg. Beat in the milk and melted, cooled butter.

2. Stir the crumbs into the milk mixture. Set aside.

3. In another bowl stir together the flours, sugar, salt, and baking powder.

4. Add grated cheese. Toss until well-coated.

5. Add milk/crumb mixture to flour mixture.

6. Stir gently by using a rubber scraper to scrape down around the sides and up through the center with a scraping/lifting/folding motion. Stir only until mostly combined—a few streaks of flour are fine.

7. Place batter in well-greased muffin pans, filling each cup ¾ full.

8. Bake in preheated 375°F oven for 12–18 minutes, until golden and springy when touched.

9. Allow muffins to cool in pan(s) for 5 minutes. Remove from pans. Serve warm, or allow to cool and freeze.

> *If I have somewhat stale Cornmeal Muffins (page 75), I pulse them in the food processor. I spread the crumbs on a baking sheet and dry them out in a just-turned-off hot oven for 5–10 minutes, stirring twice. I have used these crumbs in these muffins. The touch of onion in them with the added cheese is over-the-top-delicious.*
>
> *If you use plain bread crumbs, you could get the same basic flavor described above by adding 1–2 tsp. of grated onion along with the grated cheese.*

These are delicious on salads, soups, and casseroles, or ground up and used as dry bread crumbs.

Garlic Herb Croutons

If you want to keep it simple, you can skip the herbs and just use parsley for a little color.

MAKES: about 1½ cups

PREP. TIME: 15 minutes

BAKING TIME: 20–30 minutes

2–3 cups stale whole grain bread cubes, each about ½–1"

3–4 Tbsp. extra-virgin olive oil

½ tsp. granulated garlic

generous ½ tsp. kosher salt

fresh ground black pepper

1–2 tsp. Herbes de Provence or Italian Seasoning

1. Preheat oven to 350 degrees. Place the bread cubes in a large bowl.

2. Drizzle the oil over the cubes. Toss.

3. Sprinkle with the remaining seasonings. Toss.

4. Spread the seasoned cubes in a single layer on a half sheet.

5. Bake for 7–10 minutes until golden brown. Stir and bake again until crispy and golden, approximately 10–15 minutes. You may need to lower the temperature to prevent browning. They should be fairly dry but will crisp up more as they cool.

6. Store in a glass jar or other airtight container. If they get a bit stale, spread them on a baking sheet and put them in a hot just-turned-off oven for a few minutes to re-crisp them.

Instead of baking them, you can sauté the bread cubes over medium-low heat until they are crispy.

Other herbs that are nice here: thyme, marjoram, dill weed, ground celery seed. Or experiment with your favorite combinations.

Chocolate Bread Pudding

MAKES: 4–6 servings

PREP. TIME: 25 minutes

COOKING/BAKING TIME: 20–30 minutes

3–4 slices stale plain whole grain bread, at least 1 day old

¼ cup chopped pecans, *optional*

½ cup sugar

2 Tbsp. unsweetened cocoa powder

1 tsp. cornstarch *or* Clear Jel (not instant)

pinch salt, *optional*

1½ cups milk *or* light cream *or* combination

2 large eggs, well beaten

1–2 Tbsp. unsalted butter

1 tsp. vanilla extract

3–4 Tbsp. chocolate chips

Adding thickener suspends the cocoa in the liquid, preventing it from settling to the bottom of your pudding.

1. Cut the bread into ½–1" pieces. Loosely tossed into a measuring cup, it should measure roughly 2½ cups.

2. Place bread cubes in a well-greased 1-quart casserole. Sprinkle on the nuts and poke them in here and there.

3. Whisk the eggs in a heatproof bowl. Set aside.

4. In another bowl whisk together sugar, cocoa powder, cornstarch and optional salt.

5. Put the milk in a small, heavy-bottom saucepan. Whisk in the sugar mixture. Cook over medium heat, stirring constantly until bubbly.

6. Temper the eggs by slowly pouring hot milk mixture in a thin stream into the beaten eggs, whisking continuously until combined well.

7. Scrape around the sides and bottom of the bowl. Add the melted butter and the vanilla. Stir again.

8. Pour egg/milk mixture over bread. Poke the cubes down in so that they are all covered with liquid.

9. Bake in preheated 300°F oven for 15–25 minutes or until just set in the center. Sprinkle chocolate chips on hot bread pudding. When chocolate chips are melted, use the tines of a fork to smear them slightly on the surface. Cool on a wire rack.

10. Glaze it while still warm with ½ batch cinnamon roll glaze (see step 9 on page 214). Serve warm with milk or with thin vanilla pudding.

You may add the chocolate chips along in with the nuts.

This recipe may be halved or doubled.

Cinnamon Bread Pudding

MAKES: 4–6 servings

PREP. TIME: 25 minutes

BAKING TIME: 35–55 minutes

4 slices day-old or older cinnamon bread, *or* 2 large cinnamon rolls cut crosswise

3–4 Tbsp. cream cheese *or* butter, softened

¼-½ cup raisins *or* other dried fruit, *optional*

chopped nuts, *optional*

2 large eggs beaten

1½ cups milk, light cream, *or* combination

pinch salt, *optional*

¼ cup sugar (omit most of the sugar if using glazed cinnamon rolls)

1–2 Tbsp. butter, melted and cooled slightly, *optional*

1 tsp. vanilla extract

1. Spread the bread with as much or as little cream cheese or butter as you desire.

2. Cut into cubes ¾–1" in size.

3. Place in a well-greased 1-qt. casserole dish. Evenly distribute the optional raisins and nuts over the cubes. Poke them down in here and there.

4. In a bowl, whisk the eggs thoroughly. Whisk in milk, sugar, optional butter, vanilla, and optional salt until the sugar is dissolved.

5. Pour mixture over the prepared bread cubes, pushing down the exposed cubes to submerge them into the liquid.

6. Bake in preheated 300°F oven for 35–55 minutes or until shaky but still set in the middle.

7. Drizzle with Cinnamon Roll Glaze (see step 9 on page 214) while still quite warm. Serve warm with milk or a thin vanilla pudding.

Leftovers can be sliced and fried in a bit of butter for breakfast. You'll want to first scrape any hunks of glaze off so that they don't burn in your skillet.

To speed up the baking process, warm the milk slightly, but not so warm that it cooks the eggs on contact.

You may halve or double this recipe. Just use the appropriate size baking dish.

If you don't have leftover cinnamon bread, use regular bread. Increase the sugar to ⅓ cup and stir in ½–1 tsp. cinnamon in Step 4.

Baked French Toast

MAKES: 9" pan

PREP. TIME: 20 minutes

CHILLING TIME: 8–24 hours

BAKING TIME: 25–35 minutes

8 ounces stale whole grain bread (5–7 slices depending on the size of your bread)

3–4 Tbsp. cream cheese, softened

⅓ cup sliced almonds *or* other nuts, *optional*

¾ cup milk

6 large eggs, beaten

3 Tbsp. pure maple syrup *or* 4–5 tsp. brown sugar

Don't use heavy, dense failed bread for this recipe. Use a lighter bread that has become stale, maybe even a little dried out.

1. Spread the slices of bread with cream cheese. Cut into largish dice.
2. Place in a well-greased 8" or 9" square baking pan. Sprinkle with optional nuts.
3. Whisk together milk, eggs, and your choice of sweetener until dissolved.
4. Pour over the bread cubes.
5. Cover tightly and refrigerate 8–24 hours.
6. To bake, remove from refrigerator while oven preheats.
7. Bake in preheated 350°F oven for 25–35 minutes or until golden, puffy, and set in the middle. Serve with plain yogurt and fruit on the side, or with maple syrup or homemade syrup (page 101).

As a variation, add ½ tsp. ground cinnamon and/or a splash of vanilla extract along with the egg mixture.

VARIATIONS TO STEP 7:

• *Right before baking, sprinkle with a mixture of 2 tsp. sugar and ½ tsp. ground cinnamon.*

• *Before baking, dot or drizzle 1 Tbsp. butter over the top if you like.*

*M*y husband and I make French toast differently. I soak the bread a bit in the egg mixture so it's saturated before I fry it. He prefers the bread quickly dipped so that the egg mixture is only on the outer surface of the bread.

Simple French Toast

MAKES: 1–2 servings

PREP. TIME: 15 minutes

COOKING TIME: 5–10 minutes

3–4 slices stale whole grain bread, ½" thick

1 small egg

2 Tbsp. milk

¼ tsp. vanilla extract, *optional*

dash ground cinnamon, *optional*

unsalted butter for the skillet

1. Preheat electric skillet to 350°F. Or preheat a heavy-bottom skillet over medium heat.

2. In a mixing bowl, whisk the egg. Then whisk in milk and optional vanilla and cinnamon.

3. Put a small amount of butter in the skillet.

4. Dip the bread in the liquid, coating first one side, then the other.

5. Lay coated bread in hot, buttered skillet.

6. Fry over medium-low heat until golden brown on one side. Flip and fry on other side. Delicious topped with plain yogurt, fruit, nuts, or syrup (page 101).

Metric Conversions

If you're accustomed to using metric measurements, use these handy charts to convert the imperial measurements used in this book.

Weight (Dry Ingredients)

1 oz		30 g
4 oz	¼ lb	120 g
8 oz	½ lb	240 g
12 oz	¾ lb	360 g
16 oz	1 lb	480 g
32 oz	2 lb	960 g

Volume (Liquid Ingredients)

½ tsp.		2 ml
1 tsp.		5 ml
1 Tbsp.	½ fl oz	15 ml
2 Tbsp.	1 fl oz	30 ml
¼ cup	2 fl oz	60 ml
⅓ cup	3 fl oz	80 ml
½ cup	4 fl oz	120 ml
⅔ cup	5 fl oz	160 ml
¾ cup	6 fl oz	180 ml
1 cup	8 fl oz	240 ml
1 pt	16 fl oz	480 ml
1 qt	32 fl oz	960 ml

Oven Temperatures

Fahrenheit	Celsius	Gas Mark
225°	110°	¼
250°	120°	½
275°	140°	1
300°	150°	2
325°	160°	3
350°	180°	4
375°	190°	5
400°	200°	6
425°	220°	7
450°	230°	8

Length

¼ in	6 mm
½ in	13 mm
¾ in	19 mm
1 in	25 mm
6 in	15 cm
12 in	30 cm

Index of Tips

Index of Recipes

About the Author

I live with my husband on a small farm in southeastern Pennsylvania. We have five children, a son-in-law, a daughter-in-law, and six grandchildren.

We are both gardeners and do-it-yourselfers. Fixing, repurposing, and making items from scratch is the way things happen around here.

I also enjoy tending my flowerbeds, sewing, preserving food, learning about food, cooking nutritious meals, and all kinds of baking.

I'm involved in food service at our church and am employed part time at a local arts and crafts reuse store.

Feel free to email me any questions you might have at simpleandclassic5@gmail.com. I'll get back to you as soon as I'm able!

—Valerie Baer